CW00701123

ROOSTER – FIGHTER PILOT

From a Boyhood Dream to a Fighter Pilot

Colonel Scott Saunders, USAF (Ret)

Copyright © 2022 by Ralph Saunders, Jr.

All rights reserved. No part of this publication may be reproduced, distributed, or transmitted in any form or by any means, including photocopying, recording, or other electronic or mechanical methods, without the prior written permission of the publisher, except in the case of brief quotations embodied in critical reviews and certain other noncommercial uses permitted by copyright law. For permission requests, write to the author, addressed Attention: Permissions"at scott01s@wmconnect.com.

Colonel Scott "Rooster"Saunders, USAF (Ret)
160 Aforia Lane
Indialantic, FL 32903

Inspiration by Lieutenant Colonel Rick "Kluso" Tollini, USAF (Ret)
Cover editing by Dan Slatic
Formatting and Desktop Publishing by Keith Gildersleeve

Ordering Information: scott01s@wmconnect.com

Print ISBN: 978-1-66786-251-4

eBook ISBN: 978-1-66786-252-1

Printed in the United States of America

First Edition

Contents

Introduction

The following story is about the flying, fighting, and the professional life that I have experienced. My family life is very dear to me; however, that is a different story to tell. There will be times that family support and inspiration crossed over into my professional life, so there will be occasional references to my family in those cases. Here is a short summary of my family background.

Briefly, my father, Major General Ralph S. Saunders, Sr, USAF (Ret) was a military aviator, flying over 11,000 hours in forty years, including in World War II, the Korean War, and the Vietnam War. He flew in the B-24 Liberator bomber aircraft over the European continent from England and after victory in Europe was slated to check out in the P-51 Mustang fighter aircraft when victory in Japan brought that to a halt. My mother majored in journalism at Texas Tech, in Lubbock, TX until she married my father. They both influenced my desire to fly and to write. My first wife, Patty, gave me three wonderful children. They are Jennifer; a marvelous event planner in the heart of horse country in Northern Virginia, VA area; Scott III, an entrepreneur and founder of a unicorn company, Happy Money, with assets exceeding one billion dollars; and Matt, a multi-talented aviator, currently flying with American Airlines.

My three children have given me two grandsons and five granddaughters, from under one year to over nineteen years in age. Patty was a Registered Nurse (RN) and managed an immediate care clinic in Indianapolis. My second wife, Rhonda, whom I married after Patty passed away from cancer in 2009, is a multi-talented lady, who has done everything from soldering circuit panels in missiles, attending art school for two years, transferring those skills into the culinary field, leading to operating a catering business, becoming a chef, owning and operating a restaurant, to serving as a cardiac care technician, to working as a hospice nurse. Rhonda and I hosted all the grandchildren for a week of Glamping at River Ranch Resort, in Central Florida, with lots of fun activities.

During my lifetime, God has presented me with certain moments in time to make choices that defined me. The sum of these critical moments defines who I became. In this book I will march through those key defining moments that allowed me to become and remain a fighter pilot in heart and soul.

At the River Ranch Resort, from left to right are Rhonda Saunders, Ethan Saunders, Izzy Saunders, Caroline Rooney, Adalyn Saunders, Amelia Saunders, Catherine Rooney, and me. Evan Saunders did not make the picture because he was not yet born. (Photographer unknown, River Ranch Resort, FL, June 2019)

Chapter 1

Air Force Academy Bound

I was the oldest of three children when I lived in St. Michel housing which served the airmen and their families at Evreux-Fauville Air Base (AB) in the Normandy Region of France. In 1955, my father got in on the ground floor of the C-130A Hercules, which performs insertion and extraction of tactical forces. After having checked out in the airplane in the United States, he was assigned to the Standardization and Evaluation unit at the new C-130 base at Evreux. The fact that my father was a career pilot most likely influenced my future and that influence has flowed down in my family. My son, Matt, is not only a pilot for American Airlines but a Certified Flight Instructor (CFI). He's been giving my granddaughter Amelia flying lessons, although I had the honor of teaching her first flight lesson! Amelia and I had fun flying in my 1980 Mooney M20J, which is a four-seat, propeller driven single-engine, aircraft. Seeing her excitement as we performed climbs, turns, and descents gave me such joy. Another influencing factor to my love for flying may have been the television series, "Superman" which began airing in 1952. I must have seen a few shows on our black and white television in base housing in Sewart Air Force Base (AFB), TN before leaving for France. Whether it came from my father or Superman, I believe the spirit of flying is inherently in me because it has never left! To this day I still fly hours upon end on Angel Flights (flights where you donate your aircraft, expenses, and time to take patients to their doctors).

When I was a mere ten years old, I would repeatedly dream that I could run in an open pasture (much like the one close to where I lived in France), and if I concentrated hard enough, I would leave the earth and become airborne. I would fly over the fields, maintaining approximately 20-30 feet of altitude and 15-20 miles per hour of speed if I kept up a strong level of concentration. If I became distracted in the least, I would begin to slow down and descend. I found that if I restored my concentration level, I would regain both altitude and speed. These dreams continued for several months. I truly believe that not only did these dreams initiate my desire to fly, but they also established a pattern of how I needed to concentrate to the fullest when I flew airplanes.

I have found in over 5,200 hours of flying that there is no phase of flight or type of flying where you can lose concentration without the possibility of detrimental effects. The non-tactical aviation experts call take-off, climbs, descents, and landings the critical phases of flight, but to the tactical aviator, training missions and execution of ground attack, air combat, and student training missions are added to the list. In fact, even less than full concentration during cruise and taxi operations can be hazardous to your health and the condition of your airplane. I have been fortunate enough to have participated in all the above phases of flight. I have found, though, in over 10,000 air-to-air training engagements in the F-4D/E Phantom, Aggressor T-38A Talon, F-5E/F Tiger II, and F-15 A/B/C/D, air combat training to be likened to a three-dimensional chess match with your adversary, conducted in the x, y, and z axes. Here is a short description of the roles of these aircraft:

- T38A Talon – Twin engine supersonic trainer aircraft used by the Aggressors to simulate the Soviet M-21 fighter
- F-5E/F – Twin engine lightweight fighter aircraft, also used by the Aggressors to simulate the Soviet M-21 fighter
- F-15 A/B/C/D – Twin engine air-to-air combat aircraft that holds many time to climb records with superior weaponry and a long -range radar

What became of these dreams of flying over the fields of France by a young boy in his later life? Arriving back in the United States from France and starting the seventh grade at Surrattsville Junior High School, in Clinton Maryland, I got a fold-over pamphlet of the U.S. Air Force Academy (USAFA). That was when I decided that I would become a fighter pilot, and to do that I needed to get into USAFA. The prospect of being a cadet at USAFA was a decision I made in the 7th grade. I know this is rare, but my father having taken us kids for a visit there on our way to an overseas assignment in Okinawa probably didn't hurt.

Initially, the only thing I knew about getting admitted to USAFA through the "appointment process" was that good grades were critical. I soon learned that work ethic, extracurricular activities, good character, leadership positions, and sports participation were also key factors. While in junior high school, I delivered newspapers, and became a Boy Scout, achieving Star rank (two levels below the highest rank of Eagle Scout). I also served as a Senior Patrol Leader whose function is to oversee the four Patrol Leaders in a Scout Troop. I was overly dedicated as a Senior Patrol Leader causing me to turn in my own brother for smoking in the bathroom, which he never let me forget! In later years, I managed to mellow out a bit.

As I transitioned into high school, my father was assigned to Naha AB, on Okinawa. As I started the 9th grade at the high school there, I decided that to be a fighter pilot I had to start a full court press on all aspects required to gain an appointment. Two years later, my father was reassigned to Kadena AB, Okinawa, and I transitioned to Kubasaki High School for my final high school years. I knew I needed to do everything I could to increase my acceptance chances, so I studied hard to maintain a 3.85 grade point average and served as President of both the French Club and Junior Class. I also sold advertising and acted as Sports Editor (junior year) and Editor-in-Chief (senior year) for the 1965 Kubasaki High School yearbook, in which I was voted "Most Dependable" as one of the "superlatives" during my senior year. Among other activities to enjoy in high school, but also to build a competitive resume for my USAFA application included joining clubs, starring in the school play, running track, and winning academic awards. I also played intramural basketball and varsity football. Per the guidance of the yearbook sponsor, I had to relinquish either playing football or acting as Editor-in-Chief of the yearbook. I chose to remain Editor-in-Chief as it was more of a leadership position. Even with my schoolwork and all those extracurricular activities, I worked during the summers and after school delivering Daily Bulletins, building mechanics tool kits at the Naha AB base tool center, and lifeguarding at the Kadena Officers Club pool.

Scott Saunders

Levelland, Texas
Class Vice-Pres. 1; School Play 1; National Junior Honor Society 1; Science Club 1; French Club-Pres. 2; Class President 3; Yearbook Staff-Sports Section Editor 3; French Club-Pres. 3; NHS 3; Track 3; VFW Essay Award 3; Editor-in-chief of Yearbook 4; Election Comm., Chairman 4; Explorers.

My senior year at Kubasaki High School, Okinawa built the base foundation for an Air Force Academy appointment. (Official high school photo, Kubasaki High School, Okinawa, June 1965)

At the beginning of my senior year, it became time to apply for an appointment to USAFA. Neither myself nor my family had any ties to apply for a congressional appointment, but a son of a military person could apply for a presidential appointment, which was 100 percent competitive based on grades, extracurricular activities, and Standard Aptitude Test (SAT) scores. Taking a flight physical was also a requirement, meaning orders to Clark AB in the Philippines to take the physical examination. I took the physical where everything seemed to go well, then returned to Okinawa to finish my senior year and wait for word on my appointment. Before the end of the school year, I received a letter from USAFA stating I was qualified but didn't get an appointment with no explanation why. I knew that the primary goal of the USAFA was to produce pilots, but I didn't find out until the following year that I didn't pass the flight physical nor the reason. At that time, I knew I needed a backup plan which began with the opportunity to interview a graduate of The Citadel. He told me what to expect and I figured it would be a good preparatory school for USAFA, not only in academics but in military discipline. I applied, got accepted, and was awarded two scholarships to go there, one from the Officers Wives Club and one from Getty Oil. If I didn't serve in the military, the Getty scholarship would have to be repaid. This covered all but $150.00 of my first year at The Citadel, and I was planning on reapplying for the USAFA anyway.

The Citadel, in Charleston, SC, was rich in history, heritage, and a good foundation for either a military career or for becoming a South Carolinian businessman. I majored in physics, hoping to provide a good base for getting into USAFA. Under a very rigid fourth-class system, I worked up to being able to do 200 remedial pushups at a time, eat with my chin in, and shine shoes and shine brass and shoes to the point that you needed sunglasses to look at them. I had to be able to break down an M-1 rifle, stand in parades without passing out in the heat, and party hard on Friday nights Reapplication to USAFA required another flight physical, which I was able to take at Charleston AFB. The break of my life was during the physical when the flight surgeon measured my vertical siting height (necessary for ejection seat considerations) and said I had failed last year because I was one-half inch over the limit. He told me if I sucked my chin in a bit, I could probably get rid of the extra one-half inch, which I did, and it worked. This critical juncture in my life, solved by such a simple action of sucking in my chin, was the key to opening the door to fulfill my childhood dream of becoming a fighter pilot for the United States of America's Air Force, the best in the world!

The USAFA admissions office letter in a business envelope came to my post office box at The Citadel a few months later. Again, I was qualified but there were no vacancies. I was resigned to becoming a Citadel man and go to plan B when not more than a few weeks later, a second letter came saying that a vacancy had just opened for me, and that I should consider carefully before accepting an appointment. My response saying "YES" was sent literally within the hour. I had just achieved my first major milestone in becoming a fighter pilot!

At this point, I had realized that the first two self-guiding rules I would maintain throughout my fighter pilot life, even unto today. I later added rule #3. They are as follows:

1. *If you don't file a flight plan, you can't get a clearance,* i.e., if you really want something, you must go after it. I know some people believe

that good things will be handed to them, but that was not my philosophy at all.

2. *If you don't get something the first time you try, try again.* This rule has served me many times throughout my pursuit, as I will later point out.
3. *Eighty-twenty,* i.e., listen eighty percent of the time and speak only twenty percent of the time. You don't learn anything while you are transmitting. I adhered to this rule religiously to learn as much as I could. I had to deviate a bit as the Executive Officer for the Air Force Director of Operational Requirements at the Pentagon, where I had eleven colonel division chiefs, hungry for what the boss was expecting of them.

I finished my time at The Citadel and went to Silver City, NM at 6,000 feet (ft.) of altitude to be with my parents and grandparents for a few weeks before reporting to USAFA for basic training. This gave me the opportunity to go on runs at high altitude before transitioning to an even higher altitude of 7,200 ft. for USAFA runs. That running prep helped me during those runs during USAFA basic summer, where I was able to, along with a couple of other long-legged classmates, assist those who were less fortunate and couldn't keep up. This was probably my first real-life exposure to teamwork, critical to taking care of your wingman in combat. Soon, I said goodbye to my family, climbed on the Frontier Airlines DC-3 flight to Colorado Springs, CO to learn how to become an officer in the United States Air Force.

USAFA was vastly different from The Citadel in many ways, but there were some similarities. First, you paid to go to The Citadel along with any scholarships, but USAFA paid you one-half of a second lieutenant's salary (which at the time was $151.00 per month). However, you didn't see much of that as the cost of the uniforms, books, and savings for your graduation were deducted. The remaining amount of $10.00 a month was given to you for toiletries, incidentals, and spending money on the few days you could leave the campus.

Secondly, at USAFA you had to sign a lot of paperwork as part of your in-processing which we called "signing your life away." At The Citadel there was nothing to sign. At USAFA the school traditions were primarily migrated from West Point and the Naval Academy, as "surrogate" upper classmen were brought in at the start of USAFA in 1954. The Citadel had traditions going back to 1842 and was often called the West Point of the South.

Thirdly, USAFA was more of a "gentlemen's" institution. It was physically and academically challenging, but on a higher level. Here, cadets were required to say "Sir" once when addressing leadership, unlike The Citadel where "Sir" was required at both the beginning and end of a sentence. Also, The Citadel wasn't paid for by taxpayers, so stripping fourth classmen, also known as "knobs," of all dignity and grinding discipline into them was much easier to do than at USAFA, which was subject to congressional oversight.

Fourthly, at USAFA while eating, you sat at attention and your fork had to go directly from your plate to your mouth. At The Citadel all meals the first year were square (sitting at attention, cutting one piece of food at a time, and with each bite making a "square" motion with your hand from plate to mouth and back).

Finally, each of the institutions required memorization and had an area designed to represent their history and motivate students. At USAFA you had a small book packed with knowledge about the Air Force and its founding leaders known as your "Contrails" that you had to memorize. An important difference of USAFA for someone who wanted to be a fighter pilot was that fighter aircraft were positioned around the pavilion in the center of the Cadet area (called The Terrazzo) as a constant reminder of why we went to USAFA and what would follow. At The Citadel, you had to memorize the response to "How's the cow?" The response was, "Sir, she walks, she talks, she's full of chalk. The lacteal fluid extracted from the female of the bovine species is highly prolific to the nth degree, Sir." Charleston, SC was mostly warm. Here, cannons stood outside each battalion's barracks, reminding you of the rich army heritage of its leaders.

My first year at USAFA was relatively easy throughout the basic summer due to the discipline, physical conditioning, underwear folding practice, and shoe shining experience from The Citadel, but when the academic year began the term challenging was an understatement. My courses from The Citadel didn't transfer nor did my time. At USAFA, I was placed in over my head in advanced algebra and physics. At the end of the first quarter, I had "earned" an "F" in physics and a "D" in math. If I didn't rectify the situation, I would be out of USAFA by the end of the semester with very little chance of becoming a fighter pilot. I got to this situation by trying to learn as I did in high school by means of memorizing everything in the textbooks and regurgitating it on the tests. This technique didn't work for solving physics and math problems. My roommate and lifelong friend, Cadet Chris Lingamfelter (retired as a lieutenant colonel) found himself in a similar situation. He had even attended two years of college before his appointment. We decided to attack the problem together (Rule #2: If you don't get something the first time you try, try again). Each squadron had an assembly room that was vacant at night. Chris and I began going to that room and worked every problem in the math and physics textbooks that had the correct answers in the back of the book. In this way, we didn't memorize the words of the textbooks, but sought to understand the underlying principles of the formulae. This allowed me to bring my "F" in physics to a "C" and my "D" in math to a "B" by the end of the semester.

Plowing ahead, eventually I was able to achieve the Superintendents list (only 2-3 percent of the class get there) on a regular basis, which is a combination the Commandant's List for military aptitude and the Dean's List, for academic achievement. With a year's head start at The Citadel in academics, by my fourth year at USAFA, I had completed all my required courses and took only electives. One of which included the chance for a one-on-one with a French Air Force captain studying French history and literature.

My most relevant and useful course at USAFA for being a fighter pilot was aeronautical engineering. We learned the equations for lift, drag, and thrust, allowing us to know what conditions would give us the greatest aircraft performance and knowledge of the limits for our aircraft. During my first short four-week summer vacation, I went home to Dover AFB, where my father was the 436th Airlift Wing Deputy Commander for Operations (DO). I was at the pool when my USAFA roommate Cadet Chris Lingamfelter and his close friend, Cadet Steve Feaster came by and said, "Hello." They were at Dover AFB to catch a "hop" to Europe on a C-5 Super Galaxy cargo plane. Hops are a great bonus for military members, allowing those who aren't on orders to fly on a "space available" basis. My response was an immediate and emphatic "Yes!" I quickly grabbed a bag and all the money I had ($25.00) and joined them at the passenger terminal in less than 30 minutes.

We all got on the flight and eight hours later, we arrived at Royal Air Force (RAF) Mildenhall. After the first day, they wanted to go to Spain to see a bullfight. I didn't feel I could afford it, so I split off as a single ship. I took a train to London instead and spent an evening enjoying some night life. I soon realized that I was getting short on funds and decided to take what little money I had left and bought a train ticket to depart London and get on a road that led back to RAF Mildenhall. Once off the train I started hitchhiking, which eventually got me to my destination. Pretty much out of money, I had only had enough left for a hamburger. I caught a hop back to Dover AFB, but we had an overnight stop at Goose Bay AFB, in Labrador,

Canada. With no money at all, a first classman (4th year) from USAFA who was on the flight also helped me out. A Bachelor Officers Quarters (BOQ) room was $2.00, but I didn't have even have that. I asked the first classman if I could borrow $2.00 from him, and he gave it to me saying don't worry about paying it back. That first classman was Cadet First Class John McBroom (later Major General McBroom), who later worked my assignment back to the States from Bitburg AB, as a personnel officer in Fighter Assignments at the Military Personnel Command (MPC).

I was fortunate enough to hold the positions of 9th Cadet Squadron (CS) (Hard Core Niner) Color Bearer, 20th CS (Tough Twenty Trolls) First Sergeant, and 20th CS Squadron Commander as I navigated USAFA. I took the Pilot Indoctrination Program (PIP), earning my Private Pilot License (PPL) and whetting my voracious appetite for fighter training. Between my Second-Class (3rd year) and First-Class year, my Air Officer Commanding (AOC), Major John M. Reid, asked if I wanted to go to "SEA" (Southeast Asia) for a summer program (I was totally thinking he meant something having to do with the ocean (sea) and being on a ship. This was one of those times where choices define your destiny. I had so much discipline engrained into me that I didn't ask questions (a trait all these years later, my wife still tries to get me to change). I was very wrong in what I thought "SEA" was. Instead of the ocean, my AOC was offering me an opportunity of a lifetime to go to Southeast Asia, to fly air-to-ground combat missions in the back seat of the F-100F Super Sabre fighter jet which is capable of supersonic speeds! Like Julia Roberts said to the shop owners who wouldn't sell to her in *Pretty Woman - 1990,* "Big Mistake…Huge!" Instead of SEA, I went to Cheyenne Mountain, CO working in the 1stAerospace Control Squadron, allowing me to spend more time with my fiancé. I had just violated Rule #1: If you don't file a flight plan, you can't get a clearance. I didn't file a flight plan to go to SEA and fly fighters that was handed to me on a silver platter.

On the bright side, I worked for Bekins Van Lines, Inc., in Colorado Springs during the three weeks of my vacation as a packer and mover. It was hard work, but I earned enough for a diamond engagement ring for my fiancé, Patty, before going into Cheyenne Mountain for Operation Third Lieutenant (four weeks as a junior officer supporting space operations).

When I finally graduated from USAFA, I can't understate the joy of having my father, Air Force Colonel Ralph S. Saunders, Sr., pin a pair of gold second lieutenant bars on my shoulders. I am sure he was very proud to have a son who graduated from USAFA. I was very excited to finally be joining what we cadets always called "the Real Air Force." The graduation ceremony culminated with a flyover demonstration by the USAF Thunderbirds. At that point, I really felt like I would like to be up there in one of those loud and thunderous F-4 fighter jets. I could not wait to move out on becoming a fighter pilot.

I get my USAFA diploma from Lieutenant General Moorman, Superintendent of USAFA, launching me into the "Real Air Force." (Photographer Colonel Ralph S. Saunders, Sr., USAFA, CO, June 3, 1970)

Chapter 2

A Fighter Pilot is Born

After graduation from USAFA, it seemed forever before I could start Undergraduate Pilot Training (UPT) at Randolph AFB, in Universal City, TX. In the lottery for UPT locations, I had initially been allocated Reese AFB, in Lubbock, TX, but my new wife wanted to finish her nurses training and San Antonio had a good nursing school. I was fortunate enough to find someone who traded bases with me, giving me Randolph AFB for Reese AFB. Before UPT, we drove to Miami in our 1966 Mustang, to fly to Grand Cayman for our honeymoon. I was using the money that USAFA had held back from my salary for four years. After a week of sun, sand, sea, and snorkeling, the trek back to Universal City, TX began. We found an apartment under the approach end of Runway 15L of Randolph AFB. When the winds shifted to the northwest, Runway 33R was in use and we could feel and hear the roar of the T-38s (two-engine supersonic jet trainers) taking off in full military power right over the top of our apartment.

The first day of pilot training finally arrived in late August. My class was 72-02, or 72B, the second to last UPT Class at Randolph AFB. My first day got off to a rough start. I had the hangar number for the location, but I had trouble finding it causing me to be five minutes late. It was not a great way to start UPT. Thank goodness, we have Google directions today for maneuvering on the ground with map and time guidance. On that day, I found out that there was a Bob Saunders in our class, causing the instructors to try hard not to get us mixed up on all the paperwork. The course of instruction consisted of three phases of flying and ten academic courses. There would be two major check rides: one after flying the T-37 (a small side-by-side two-engine slow jet trainer), and one after the T-38.

The first phase was Light Plane and consisted of 18 hours in the T-41 (military version of the Cessna-172 single-engine propeller driven basic General Aviation (GA) aircraft but with a more powerful engine) for USAFA graduates who took the Pilot indoctrination Program (PIP). Basic was 90 hours in the T-37 and finally 120 hours in the T-38. The course was set to last 53 weeks.

Getting ready to fly the T-38. 72-02 or 72B was the second to last UPT squadron at Randolph AFB. (Photographer unknown, Randolph AFB, TX, circa mid-1971)

The T-41 flying was not difficult, as I already had a private pilot license from PIP. During basic, the flying was more challenging with instrument flying being introduced. I excelled in the contact phase (takeoffs, landings, and maneuvers), because I naturally took to flying the airplane, using the laws of aerodynamics I had learned at USAFA. The instrument flying was a different story. On the T-37 instrument check, a strong crosswind during holding (flying a somewhat elliptical racetrack pattern while you waited your turn to start an approach to the field) threw me a curve ball. I ended up losing points for not maintain the holding pattern track.

During primary phase, the flying was again highly satisfactory for the contact phase and formation flying. I was quickly able to observe what I was supposed to do and execute the maneuvers after a couple attempts. After practicing diligently, I felt confident I'd mastered the maneuvers. Not my lucky day, while taking my final contact check there was a 10-knot tailwind, and the tower hadn't changed runways to account for the high winds. This caused me to land long (land further down the runway than required) on the no-flap landing and lose points. The Academic Phase saved my bacon allowing me to finish 8th in the class out of 25 students. This phase consisted of ten different aeronautical knowledge topics each terminating with 100 question tests. Out of 1,000 questions, I only missed two, winning me the Academic trophy and First Place in my class in academics!

With pilot training nearly complete, we prepared for the pre-pick of our aircraft assignments. The Class Commander gave us a list of available aircraft, one for each member of the class. After a couple of days, we gathered in the squadron conference room. The pilot first in class had the first pick. Flying scores made up 50 percent and Academic standing made up the other half. Although I was first in academics, my holding in the T-37 and my no-flap tailwind landing in the T-38 brought me down to the 8th position. There was only one sure fighter assignment and that was the A-7 (a subsonic, ground attack jet workhorse aircraft). After that, there was a choice of an F-106/F-4 (the F-106 was a single-engine jet air defense interceptor aircraft). The number seven pilot in the pre-pick wanted a WC-135 (special mission aircraft to collect atmospheric samples), which would have left me with the last fighter. Much to my dismay, the WC-135 assignment was to Rota AB, Spain and his wife wanted to stay in the U.S. for her nursing career. The next closest choice of a fighter appeared to be a T-33, which was a base support single-engine jet aircraft that had previously been used to train new pilots in the Air Force. The T-33 assignment was to the 31st Tactical Fighter Wing (TFW) at Homestead AFB near Miami, FL. Following a hunch and using Rule #1: *If you don't file a flight plan, you can't get a clearance,* I took the initiative of calling the Deputy Commander for Operations (DO) of the 31st TFW and explained my desire to fly fighters. I asked if the T-33 assignment could lead to an F-4 at Homestead. He urged me to come on down and said he would do everything he could to get me into one of his F-4s in 6 to 12 months. I took that as a "go" and accepted the T-33 to Homestead.

Our mission in the T-33 was Base Flight Support. At that time in the Air Force, pilots were required to fly a minimum number of hours each year to collect flight pay. For those pilots in desk jobs, the T-33 was a good aircraft to log those hours. The T-33 was a two-seat aircraft that we always flew with two pilots. I always volunteered to fill the second seat with the pilots who needed their minimum flight hours. I learned a lot from pilots like Lieutenant Colonel Jarvis, Chief of Air Force Recruiting for Florida who had 5,500 hours of fighter time, having flown two back-to-back combat tours in the F-105 Thunderchief (heavy single engine, high speed ground attack fighter). There used to be a fighter pilot saying that if you built a runway all the way around the world, Republic would build an airplane that would use it. Republic built the F-105.

He was short three hours of night time, with which I offered to assist. He was able to get it all in one flight by initially flying a cruise climb (increase your altitude by climbing as your weight was reduced by burning fuel) tall the way to Jacksonville, FL up to an altitude of 37,000 ft. He then turned south in a very shallow 15-degree bank turn to conserve energy. Finally, he started a maximum range descent (starting a descent at the exact distance from your destination to begin a glide to the field at best glide speed and save the most fuel) at just the right distance to make it back to Homestead AFB with sufficient fuel for landing. He even switched off the aircraft heat because it used up some of the precious fuel. This was a huge accomplishment with the available fuel in our T-33. I followed his lead and executed this object lesson many times later in my career. Once was when I flew 1,025 miles from Colorado Springs to New Orleans with the help of a tailwind. The second time was over the South China Sea to get my number four wingman on the ground at destination successfully, with sufficient fuel remaining for landing the aircraft on a flight from Thailand to the Philippines. I will go into more details of this harrowing incident later. Flying the T-33 was a good way to hone my instrument skills, because you had to monitor your heading frequently since the wings were warped, probably from the abuse of student pilots pushing the aircraft beyond operating limits. Homestead AFB had two of the very oldest T-33s in existence, 1957 and 1958 models.

My additional duty when not flying was to assist the Wing Weapons Officer, Captain Will Rudd. As a first lieutenant, I didn't yet perform major impact duties. Our office symbol was DOW, Directorate of Weapons. I made my office symbol DOWSP; i.e., Directorate of Weapons *Spare Part*. This assignment was an excellent introduction into flying in an Air Force unit as well as my first real Air Force staff experience.

As a new initiative, I planned and supervised a mission for our support enlisted personnel to get a flight in the Base Flight T-29 (a twin-engine propeller driven aircraft used in commercial aviation known as the DC-3). The T-29 transport aircraft took them to Avon Park Bombing and Gunnery Range in Central Florida, which was used by fighter units based at Homestead AFB and MacDill AFB, FL. The purpose was to familiarize the support personnel with the operational mission of the F-4 Phantom aircraft they supported. Another important mission I was assigned was to fly a rare blood type up to Maxwell AFB, AL for a patient who needed it for an operation. The blood was a hard requirement due to the rare blood type, needed for a patient to survive a critical surgery. Ground transportation couldn't deliver it quickly enough, so they brought it to me in a small cooler and I was able to fly it up to Alabama in time for the operation. I guess this was my first "Angel Flight," of which there will be more later.

I experienced my first aircraft breakdown in the T-33 while flying with another lieutenant in a round-robin (out and back) to Patrick AFB, also located on the east-coast of Florida. As luck would have it, when we got there the standby attitude indicator and heading indicator became inoperative. We flew under Instrument Flight Rules (IFR) in the Air Force. Today, I would have called back for permission to bring the plane home under Visual Flight Rules (VFR), being able to survive without those two instruments by using an aeronautical map and dead reckoning. With my limited experience at that time, I took a more conservative route and got a night at the temporary quarters on the beach at Patrick while we waited for the repair. We each bought a swimsuit and a toothbrush and chilled on one of the best beaches in

Central Florida for a day. While flying the T-33, I had enough spare time for other activities, one of which was to build plastic fighter models. On the weekends we went boating in our ski boat and even took a road trip to Key West, with now Lieutenant Chris Lingamfelter and his wife Lui, spearing lobsters under the Seven Mile Bridge on U.S. 1. Later, I took my wife waterskiing in our ski boat, she let go of the rope because she could not get up. It was a good thing, because the next week we found out she was pregnant with our daughter, Jennifer!

When many of my USAFA and UPT classmates came to Homestead AFB for water survival training, we would go out in the boat. In one boating adventure that started at sunset, Lieutenant Mick Davey (classmate from USAFA) and I went lobster fishing on the first night of lobster season. Armed with flashlights and fishing nets we drove the boat to the shallow waters close to Miami Beach and caught seven lobsters (no easy feat!) We scanned the bottom of the water in and around the waterways of Miami beach looking for their beady eyes reflecting up at us. Before they could scurry away, we quickly submerged our nets and scooped them up.

An officer of Florida Fish and Wildlife met us at the boat ramp just after sunrise. He measured each lobster with his measuring device and found them all to be approximately one-half inch short. So much for having eyeballed the legal limit. Instead of a ticket with a costly fine, he only issued a warning, saying he was taking them to a children's orphanage ..yeah right, I'll bet they ended up on his table! Tired, hungry, and with no lobsters, we changed into work clothes for a long day ahead.

In the evenings I also had time to take GA flight instructor training and get my CFI (Certified Flight Instructor) rating. Getting a CFI rating involves taking a written test on aeronautical knowledge, having a Designated Pilot Examiner (DPE) grill you for hours on your aircraft systems and the Federal Aviation Administration (FAA) rules and regulations, and taking a practical test. During the practical, you fly with a DPE, and you "teach" him how to perform all the maneuvers including doing practice emergency situations. The whole process usually takes six or more months. The phenomenon called "rites of passage" hit me hard, meaning nearly every CFI fails their first check ride, and I was no different. Implementing Rule #2, *If you don't get something the first time you try, try again.* I passed on my second attempt and have flown over 800 hours of instruction in GA since then. With my 3,800 hours of Air Force flying time, my total hours are now over 5,200 hours. As promised, I was called into the DO's office six months after arriving at Homestead AFB and told I was going into the 307th Tactical Fighter Squadron (TFS) to upgrade into the F-4.

This was the realization of my dreams at last, and I can't overstate how excited I was! I was even so gung-ho that I quickly had the 307th TFS patch sewn on all my flight suits. I got all the aircraft manuals and regulations that I needed and joined the class for the first hour of academics. After about fifteen minutes, there was a knock on the door. The DO poked his head in and motioned for me to come out into the hallway. What he told me was that Headquarters USAF MPC had told him, that he didn't have the authority to place students on his own accord into the formal F-4 Replacement Training Unit (RTU) course. I was told to return to T-33 base flight operations and wait, which is what I did. With huge disappointment, I changed all the patches back on my flight suits and reported back to my old position. Time for Rule 2: *If you don't get something the first time you try, try again.* Six months later, I had flown a T-33 to Oakland International Airport, CA to have a new and more accurate altimeter installed in the airplane.

My parents lived on Travis AFB CA, not far from Oakland. I had precoordinated to visit with them after dropping off the T-33 and before flying commercial back to Miami, FL. During the visit my parents got a call, but the person calling was trying to reach me, not my parents. To my surprise, I was told one of the students slated for an F-4 RTU class at MacDill AFB in Tampa, FL had broken his leg and there was an open slot! They asked me if I could accept it because the class had already started the previous week. I said there would be no problem because I already had the first week's lesson of emergency procedures memorized. Bummer for the guy with the broken leg, but finally almost 12 months to the day of my bitter RTU start, I was officially in!

When I got off the phone, I booked a red eye. commercial flight to Miami for that evening. My colleague, Captain Bruce Kreidler and I left from Homestead AFB early the next morning towing my boat. The following week, he brought his boat up from Homestead AFB. We arrived in academics by 2:00 p.m. in the afternoon at MacDill AFB. I decided not to bring my Yamaha 350 motorcycle, selling it at Homestead. I liked to ride my motorcycle fast WAY before Tom Cruise did it in *Top Gun-1986*. I loved to ride the back roads around Homestead AFB. One day, as in *TOP Gun – 1986,* I thought to myself, "I feel the need for speed,"and I rode 62 miles from Homestead AFB to Fort. Lauderdale on Interstate 95 (I-95, Death Highway), just to go to the beach. It ended up being my only motorcycle, as I became a new father while at MacDill AFB and wanted to spend more time with our new daughter.

Another colleague, Captain Russ Wisanen, accepted my Power of Attorney and out-processed me from Homestead AFB allowing me to stay for classes. I went back two weeks later to pick up my 1966 Mustang and my wife. I also said thanks and goodbye, as my unit gave us a going away party.

F-4 RTU was both demanding and exhilarating. On my very first flight the maintainers dropped the wing tanks. We then flew the F-4 at its maximum speed of Mach 2.2, which is equivalent to 1588 mph. Our flight was out over the Gulf of Mexico in one of the Warning Areas. We climbed to 41,000 ft. in full afterburner, nosed over (lowering the nose to increase speed), flying in a slight descent to 37,500 ft. of altitude, then leveled off, accelerating to Mach 2.2. This was the optimum flight path for attaining maximum speed. We flew to 150 miles from MacDill AFB in a matter of minutes. Then we banked into almost a 90-degree bank turn, pulled full aft stick (pulling back on the control stick to increase the pitch attitude of the aircraft) to decelerate, and returned to base. As the jet decelerated the "g" forces increased, we had to release backward pressure on the control stick at 6 "gs" on the g-meter to keep from overstressing the aircraft going through Mach tuck (when the F-4 aircraft transitions from supersonic to subsonic speed, the nose pitches up suddenly, adding two to three "gs" to the aircraft, overstressing it).

We had just burned through all the fuel available for a mission with just enough to return safely to base. This was an object lesson on the capabilities of the aircraft and the rapid depletion of fuel in full afterburner, which were useful for future flying of the aircraft.

Follow-on flying included landings, maneuvers, instruments, night operations, bombing, strafing (shooting ground targets from a low altitude three-degree firing pass), basic fighter maneuvers, air-to-air refueling, air combat maneuvers, navigation on cross-country flying, and formation flying. We also received academics on aircraft and weapons systems operations to round out our preparation for operating a combat aircraft. Particularly challenging operations during my training included formation takeoffs, air-to-air refueling, and bombing.

During formation takeoffs, you had to maintain both the same speed as your leader and wing-tip clearance between your aircraft and his as the two aircraft accelerated to takeoff speed down the runway. You then rotated to the takeoff attitude as close to the same time as the leader did, to not fall behind during the takeoff. All this was accomplished initially with throttle modulation and rudder control. Once airborne, you could use your ailerons and elevators. I had often practiced formation takeoffs in the T-38, but this was much more demanding with the increased thrust plus the size of the aircraft.

Successful air-to-air refueling, required you to fly from the observation position (ninety degrees left or right of the tanker aircraft and above its altitude) on the wing of the KC-135 (a military version of the B-707, with a refueling boom that extends from the back of the aircraft to transfer fuel to receivers) aircraft to a trail formation position behind and under the boom (long tube with small wings on the end to stabilize it) of the tanker aircraft. Then continuously flew precise formation with the tanker, moving forward and up very slowly until the boomer "plugged" your air refueling receptacle with the nipple at the end of the boom. Director lights on the fuselage of the tanker directed you up and down and forward and back to stay in position. You flew this precise position until you received all your fuel. Later, during combat missions in Southeast Asia with 12 MK 82 bombs (500 lbs. each), I had to put one engine in minimum afterburner and modulate the other throttle to overcome the additional weight of the aircraft to stay in the refueling position.

Bombing was a challenge because you needed to consider wind, dive angle, and airspeed to release your bombs at the exact second to get them as close to the target as possible. This had to be done at either a 15-degree dive angle or at a 30-degree dive angle. At first 30 degrees of dive seemed like you were setting yourself up to hit the ground. On all my combat missions, I had to get used to 45 degrees of dive, which at first really seemed straight down. If you released your bombs by depressing a small button on your control stick called the pickle button at the correct altitude and started a recovery pull up, everything was fine. At the Avon Park Bombing and Gunnery Range we flew a box pattern around the target taking turns dropping our practice bombs. One day as we practiced a 30-degree dive bomb pass, the number 2 pilot "pressed" (releasing below the planned release altitude) on a bomb pass to get a better solution. What resulted was a rooster tail when his aircraft came close enough to the ground to kick up a cloud of dust into the air. Each time we came off the target, we had to announce it on the radio. In this case, the number two man, after a long delay in a weak voice called "two's off." This was an object lesson that "pressing" could be hazardous to the health of you, as well as your aircraft.

Night flying was probably the most relaxed phase of the course. We didn't practice air combat or bombing at night, but merely had to takeoff, land, and fly formation. The work schedule involved going to work at 5:00 p.m., brief, preflight, and take-off after sunset, usually finishing by midnight. After sleeping in one day, I was cruising up and down the Hillsborough River in Tampa FL in my ski boat when a couple of very tall men motioned me to come over to their hotel dock. I went over and they asked me if I could give them a ride, and I said, "Sure, why not?" After the ride, they asked me if I wanted two free tickets to their performance that night. It turned out that they were part of the Harlem Globetrotters. How great was it that I gave two of the World-Famous Harlem Globetrotters a ride in my boat! I was grateful for the ticket gesture but thanked them and told them I had to fly that night.

I flew my required F-4 cross country flight in the back seat, under the "hood" vision restricting device to demonstrate my ability to fly solely on instruments. We flew west of the Mississippi to Colorado with an empty napalm can fashioned as a baggage pod, to bring back Coors beer for the squadron, as it was not yet for sale east of the Mississippi. The only problem was that one of the wing fuel tanks didn't feed from the wing up to the engine fuel control system. My instructor, the squadron weapons officer quickly calculated that we could still make the trip. That was easy for him to say because he didn't have to deal with the asymmetric (unevenly balanced left side versus right side) loading on the airplane. I trimmed out the aircraft as much as I could, then struggled to fly to Colorado and back to give the troops the delicacy of Coors beer. The baggage pod was large enough to bring back 16 cases plus 6 six-packs of the highly desirable refreshment. (Some things you never forget!)

While attending F-4 RTU, I was able to use my CFI certificate for the first time. The Air Force began accepting navigators in lieu of pilots in the back seats of the F-4. The position was known as the Weapons System Operator or WSO. My WSO for my RTU course was Lieutenant Jim Taft, who wanted to get his Private Pilot License (PPL). Jim and I would go to the GA airport after work where I trained him in the Yankee single-engine aircraft. He continued his pursuit of commercial aviation and eventually flew as an airline captain for American Airlines. I had to stop my instruction after work during his course to get his pilot's license, because I became a brand-new father, and couldn't continue two flying endeavors at the same time. I was really excited about being a father, and fatherhood took priority over giving lessons. I got to come home after flying the F-4 all day and hold my baby girl! Life was good!

At the end of the course, I received my next assignment to the 13th TFS Panther Pack at the Udorn Royal Thai Air Force Base (RTAFB). The war in Southeast Asia was still on, and I was going to be a part of it. I drove cross-country to get on a transport airplane at Travis AFB to fly to Thailand for the beginning of a one-year tour in the F-4D and F-4E.

F-4 RTU at MacDill AFB, Tampa, FL. My WSO, Lieutenant Jim Taft, was also my first student, who later flew for American Airlines. (Photographer unknown, MacDill AFB, FL, circa 1973)

Chapter 3

Combat in Southeast Asia

Upon arrival at Udorn RTAFB, in the town of Udon Thani, which is a northern town in Thailand, not far from the Laotian border, the first thing to hit me was the heat, figuratively and literally. It was a combination of high temperatures with high humidity. It was the first time in my life that I could sweat standing still! I soon found out that, besides the fact that air conditioning was installed nearly everywhere, the next best step for beating the heat was to not wear your Nomex flight suit when you were not flying. To solve the problem of what to wear when not flying, I was directed to go see the "Thief." He was called that because he had a lock on all the unofficial clothing requirements of the aviators on the base. The first chance I got; I was off to the "Thief" whose "store front" was less than 100 yards from the main gate. I bought several "work suits" which were tailored cotton one-piece jump suits complete with embroidered rank, name, and unit patches. I also purchased the mandatory party suit, very similar to the work suit, but it was black rather than olive drab green and you only needed one for occasional parties or celebrations. The party suit would be useful even when returning to the "World," which was what we all called the United States.

I was assigned a two-person room in the 13th TFS "hooch," which was a makeshift building with a common latrine and shower, bunk beds and, most importantly, a window air conditioner. My wife made blackout curtains for both windows for me and my roommate, Lieutenant Vince Evans. This was critical, because D Flight in the 13th TFS, provided Udorn's first fighters on the targets at 6:00 a.m. every day, which meant daytime sleep was essential. For liquid and solid nourishment, it was only a two-minute walk to the Officers Club.

For $10.00 each per month, we paid a maid to clean our room, shine our boots, and wash our clothes in the "klong," or ditch filled with water near our hooch. Consequently, all our underwear turned orange, requiring them to be replaced when we returned to the "World."

At the squadron, my additional duties started at the bottom of the totem pole, as the junior pilot in the squadron and D Flight. I arrived at Udorn RTAFB as a lieutenant. Since Vince was also my WSO, we became the only lieutenant "formed crew" at Udorn. The squadron leadership believed in us and gave us the honor of flying together! It was great! I had also joined the F-4 community as one of the first pilots to start in the front seat as an aircraft commander without having to go through a tour in the back seat first.

When I wasn't flying, my job was to collate and staple flight publications, paint baseboards in the squadron building, and perform other similar tasks. As I gained seniority and made captain, I got an additional duty of working in Wing Scheduling Operations. This entailed scheduling Chandy Range, KC-135 refueling tankers and the C-130 Duckbutt support (airborne rescue support) for the transit flights of our F-4s to go from Udorn to Tainan AB, Taiwan for depot overhaul, and to Clark in the Philippines for live missile firing, known as Combat Sage.

We went back and forth to the squadron and the non-flight line side daily or sometimes twice-daily on a 28-passenger blue Air Force bus that ran continuously from one side of the base to the other. Sometimes Eldridge, our real live meat-eating Black Panther mascot and his handler, a lieutenant in the squadron, would also use the bus for transportation.

I am preparing for one of my 25 combat missions in the F4-D at Udorn RTAFB. (Photographer unknown, Udorn RTAFB, Thailand, circa August 1973)

I flew 25 combat missions between mid-June, when I arrived, until August 14, 1973. The date was significant, because it was the day before the last day of hostilities in SEA. My time to drop on the target or TOT was usually 6:00 a.m. down south, which meant showing up at the squadron at 11:30 p.m. the night before for intelligence briefings, review of the Rules of Engagement (ROE), and a briefing of the Search and Rescue (SAR) procedures. This was followed by flight briefings, crew briefings, suiting up into our "g" suits (special suits to compress the body to counter the effects of the massive "g's we'd pull), strapping on our .38 caliber revolvers, and stuff two frozen water bottles in our "g" suit pockets. Then we pre-flighted the aircraft, took off, joined up, and flew to the tanker on the Hickory track (air-to-air stationary refueling track at 25,000 ft. of altitude). We refueled, flew to the target area, rendezvoused with the Forward Air Controller (FAC), and dropped our bombs on the target.

The return flight consisted of flying back to base on a direct path if we had expended all 12 bombs on one pass and had sufficient fuel. If not, we got some post-strike refueling on the Hickory track. In either case, the frozen water bottles were just the right temperature for drinking on the return to base. Then we landed, debriefed with maintenance and intelligence, and finally debriefed with our two-ship flight crew. A typical combat flight, with pre-strike and post-strike refueling was three hours in length, which summed up my 25 combat missions to yield to 75 hours of combat time earning me an Air Medal.

Vince and I often went to work and back to the hooch twice a day. We existed on two four-hour sleep cycles because our flight, "D" flight was first on target down south every day, at sunrise. We went to work at 11:30 p.m. at night to fly and then again at 1:00 p.m. to do additional duties. During the first time of the day when we retreated to the non-flight line side of the base, we relaxed at the pool, played tennis, ate breakfast, and slept. During the second time of the day, we went to the bar, ate, and slept until 11:00 p.m. We kept this cycle up until August 15, 1973, the last day of air combat in Southeast Asia.

There were a few missions of note during my tour at Udorn. Vince and I usually flew on the wing of Major Phil Drew. He had shot down a North Vietnamese Mig-17 in his F-105 with his gun during his first tour which was quite an accomplishment on a ground attack mission. One day, we got assigned a target of a boat that was loaded with munitions, sailing down the Mekong River. When we located the boat with our FAC's assistance, Major Drew flew the first pass but didn't take out the target.

Our normal bomb pass was to roll in from 13,000 ft. at a 45-degree dive angle and place the pipper (center dot) on our pre-computed aim point offset for wind from the desired impact point of the bombs. The milliradians, or mills of depression from the boresight (center radial) of the aircraft, that were computed during flight planning were dialed into our bomb sights. The FAC provided estimated winds on the ground location of the desired impact point. As another reference we would also look at his smoke from the rockets he fired at the target and the direction and intensity of any drifting from his mark.

We then added wind drift to the equation of the aim point. As we proceeded down the "chute" on our dive pass we made final adjustments to ensure we did not have any bank or "g" on the airplane at the time of release, which would induce errors into the path of the bombs. The goal was to release at 7,000 ft. and pull out by 4,500 ft. thus avoiding small arms fire. During the pull out, after jinking (rapidly changing your flight path in two different directions to confuse enemy fire), and once the nose was above the horizon, we could bank slightly to see if we had hit our target. The FAC might give us some feedback, or we would get results back at the squadron.

When it came time for my pass, I rolled in, had a good run down the chute, and got a good release. When I pulled off the target, starting my climb, I looked back. and saw that my bombs had exploded just behind the boat. I later learned that two additional two-ship flights had attacked the same target without success. Finally, around noon a two-ship from Ubon RTAFB was sent against the boat with laser guided bombs and achieved success (they "shacked" the target; i.e., hit it dead center). I realized later I had a perfect solution for an anchored boat but alas I neglected to account for boat motion. I also learned that I knocked out his rudder, so at least I didn't miss the target completely.

Another interesting mission happened when I flew on the wing of our squadron commander, Lieutenant Colonel Keith Lukens. This was his second combat tour in SEA, having flown his first in the F-105. On this day, our target was a weapons storage site with a distinctive red tile roof. We arrived in the vicinity of the target but there was partial cloud cover, making it difficult to see the ground. Lieutenant Colonel Lukens located the target just after passing over the top of it. I was flying close formation because we had not split up yet to make separate passes. My lead then rolled over on his back and started pulling inverted toward the target, performing the back half of a Cuban Eight maneuver resulting in a 60-degree dive angle. I hung in there on the wing, following his maneuvers lock step. When his bombs came off his aircraft, I released mine. As we pulled off the target, we realized that we had not only hit the target but observed secondary explosions from the weapons stored within the building. There was no need that day for an aim point with a 60-degree dive angle. I thought that a 45-degree pass was steep. Sixty degrees honestly looks straight down! We had the good fortune of an amazing pass and came off target with the satisfaction that we had earned our keep that day!

The final mission of note was a four-ship deployment from Udorn, across South Vietnam, over the South China Sea, to Clark AB in the Philippines for Combat Sage's live firing of air-to-air missiles to test the missiles and train the crews. I was the flight lead, and my number three man was deputy lead. During the flight briefing, I learned that my airplane was still on the test stand all torn apart. It had experienced major maintenance and the rear ejection seat was even out of the airplane. We had a hard tanker rendezvous time and our C-130 Duckbutt rescue support was also locked in. I coordinated with maintenance to put all the resources possible to get my aircraft in the air, including the support of myself and my back seater Vince.

I briefed my deputy lead to take the three-ship to the tanker and wait for me no longer than one hour. That was all the slack we had. I briefed him that if I was not there in one hour that he should take the three-ship to Clark AB without me. The crew van took us to the airplane at the test stand near the end of the runway, and our task was clear ..get that airplane put back together! As the maintenance crew replaced each component in the aircraft, and Vince and I bolted the panels back on with speed handles (a hand tool with bits that operated much faster than a conventional screwdriver). Those were the days before battery powered drills loaded with the proper bits. Ultimately, we got the airplane rebuilt and in the air with enough time to join our three wingmen. Trading fuel for speed, we hightailed it to the tanker arriving exactly one hour late. I took back the lead of the four-ship. As I was coming off the boom from getting my gas, I asked if anyone needed to top off their fuel tanks. Once again, as in *Pretty Woman - 1990*, "Big Mistake...Huge!" I should have done a standard fuel check and decided for myself, which I discovered when we had departed the tanker. Vince and I calculated that we could make Clark AB if we cruise-climbed to 37,500 ft. as we burned off our external fuel from our wing tanks and started a max range descent into Clark at the correct distance out. We did in fact get all that done. We even had to cheat just a little when we reported our altitudes passing in the descent to Manila Air Traffic Control (ATC). The weather was good with no clouds, and I didn't want us to have to land short of Clark AB at the Manila International Airport, because that would have been super embarrassing. The same would have been true having to return to Udorn RTAFB before passing the half-way point.

We got our low man, number four wingman, our very own Blue Four, over the field, on initial (overhead the runway numbers, just before turning downwind in the traffic pattern), with 1,500 lbs. of fuel, which is the exact minimum fuel for arrival at the field. As revealed earlier, I had learned this technique from a seasoned F-105 pilot while flying the T-33. I used this technique later in the F-15 to "stretch" gas. The F-15 with turbofan versus turbojet engines "made" fuel at the higher altitudes. I even use it in my Mooney, getting fuel consumption down to 6.9 gallons per hour. After August 15th, we had some interesting times at Udorn, as we no longer flew ground attack combat missions. Initially, our squadron was assigned an air superiority mission. This required training in air-to-air combat. Thus, we trained in Basic Fighter Maneuvers (BFM) and Air Combat Maneuvers (ACM). Much to our chagrin we got switched back to a ground attack role a few months later, even though our squadron had achieved many kills during the war with minimum losses. Now, we had to train in ground attack after the war using peacetime procedures.

We learned that our unit was scheduled to get an Operational Readiness Inspection (ORI) (a higher headquarters examination of everything a wing does in its combat mission). The kicker was that the evaluation parameters were to be those of stateside, peacetime procedures, i.e., 30-degree high dive and 15-degree low angle dive bomb. None of us had flown those parameters since RTU. All our bombing had been at 45 -degree dive angle passes. No big surprise that we didn't pass with acceptable scores, but you never want to be in a unit that has failed an ORI!

Everything you do is looked at under a microscope as you get ready for the retest. Well into the training for the revisit, we switched back to our familiar 45-degree dive angle passes with the logic that if hostilities resumed that would be what we would use. This time we passed with flying colors. We knew our stuff! During the war, Captain Don Colpitts, on his second combat tour, had an inoperative gun sight one a mission. He was able to get his bombs on target with no reticle on his windscreen, using only the "sight picture" (looking at the target and visualizing where the pipper would have been). That is what I call some bombing! We had an interesting time in December 1973 during the fuel crisis. For a month we only had enough fuel to spare for aircraft commanders to keep up their landing currency.

Essentially without jobs, the squadron met at 7:30 a.m. for roll call to make sure everyone was still in one-piece from any activities the night before. After we had breakfast together and were cleared off for the rest of the day, our focus was our tennis games and suntans by the pool. The Thai annual Waterfall Festival also happened in December, when we had too much time on our hands. The tables in the club were lined up in a long row and soaked down with water, so that we could get a running start and flop down on the first table with enough energy to slide to the other end of the tables. We called this exercise "carrier landings." Kids today call it "slip and slide," doing it on the ground. Some kids never grow up, which is the nature of being a fighter pilot, I guess. Thank goodness this feat ended with no major injuries.

This was not the case though, at the first annual Panther Pack golf weekend at Kon Kaen, Thailand. Before the end of the war, only a small number of pilots could leave the base at any one time because we always had to fill the daily target list, or Fragmentary Order (FRAG Order). Now that the war was over, this gave our operations officer the opportunity to plan and execute a weekend getaway for the entire squadron. We proceeded on buses for an hour to Khon Kaen Resort for a golf match and a banquet. We all had rental golf clubs and caddies, with one caddy designated to carry enough beer in a golf bag to keep everyone happy.

The golf was fun, and the banquet went well up to the point when someone in our group threw a cocktail glass across the room from where one-half us were sitting. It struck the floor, bounced up, and hit Vince in the leg cutting him open. I got him into a taxi and took him to a local Thai doctor's office. The good news was that he took us in at night and even had a University of Chicago Medical School certificate on the wall. The bad news was that he had no antiseptic, so he poured a half a bottle of whiskey on Vince's leg before he stitched him up. This despicable act is known in the fighter pilot community as "alcohol abuse."

Another major injury occurred when Eldridge, our Black Panther, was riding on the bus one day with his handler from the flight line to the support side of the base. For no reason, Eldridge decided to take a chunk out of a Thai woman's leg on the bus. Since the war was over, this incident could not be ruled out as a combat-related injury or "friendly fire," so Eldridge got life imprisonment in the Phoenix Zoo.

One of my last duties at Udorn RTAFB was to serve as range officer at the Chandy Range. As the wing scheduler for Chandy Range, I had been exempted, but now it was my time in the barrel. After we had finished combat operations, it finally became my turn for a tour. The function of the range officer was to control the flights from all over Thailand that came to the bombing and gunnery range and to keep them safe. They also made sure their scores were properly recorded and transmitted back to their bases. Chandy Range was in the middle of the country, giving equal access to all the fighter wings. To get there without my F-4 Phantom, I took the "Klong," which was a C-130 "taxi" that flew a circular route around the country every day. The Klong took me to Korat RTAFB, adjacent to the small town of Lop Buri, Thailand.

My first day of duty was exciting, because my driver took me to the observation tower while a flight was strafing their target. The detachment commander, a major, got very excited because the driver put us at risk by driving on the road adjacent to live fire from the strafing fighters! My one-week tour only got better after that. Sitting as range officer was not terribly exciting if all the pilots flew a good pattern and didn't "press." Again, pressing is flying below the release altitude to try for a better score, i.e., getting your bombs closer to the bullseye.

When off duty, I had a hotel room in the town of Lop Buri, which was a very scenic location. I was able to walk around the town, seeing how the local citizens led their daily lives. I saw a Buddhist shrine, ate the local Thai food, and witnessed a wedding party procession. The procession consisted of five pickup trucks with the bride and groom in the lead pickup truck. After my week at the range, I was able to ride the Klong down to Bangkok, only 75 miles south of Korat, for a couple of days of Rest and Relaxation (R&R) before heading back to Udorn.

All in all, our squadron was fortunate enough not to lose anyone to a fatal accident in the twelve months that I was there. Just before I had arrived a squadron pilot had to eject from a distressed aircraft just before reaching Udorn into a jungle with hostile locals. For his sake, he didn't have to use his firearm and he was picked up. We had one back seater, Lieutenant Marty Simek, who carried a large knife strapped to his leg on every mission! He picked up the nickname "Blade," but as tough as that made him sound, it wasn't practical. He'd have had an interesting time if he had to eject from his aircraft. We knew we could be subject to small arms fire, but we could not see the bullets during the day. We "jinked," or made a rapid change in our flight path coming off the target anyway to minimize exposure and to give any SA-7 heat seeking missile shooters a more difficult time. We normally didn't descend below 4,500 ft. because it took special permission to go below that altitude to strafe. You also had to be in a F-4E which had the gun and have enemy troops in contact.

We flew nearly every day before August 15th, 1973. After that there was occasional time off for visits to Pattaya Beach, Bangkok, Bellows Air Force Station (AFS) beach in Hawaii, and even back to the "World."

I had the occasion to visit my parents on leave over the Christmas holidays, because I had enough seniority having arrived in June. Shortly after getting there and relaxing a bit, my father, who was 60th Military Airlift Wing (MAW) Commander at the time, asked me if I wanted to accompany him on a trip to Europe in the C-5. This was great! Flying while on vacation! Of course, I said yes. We took off from Travis AFB, CA for Hill AFB, UT to pick up a loading dock to transport to Ramstein AB, GE. Flying the C-5 was much different than flying the F-4. I got to make two landings at Travis AFB before we started the trip but landing the C-5 is like landing a two-story apartment building. You don't have to worry about crosswinds, though, because, even if the airplane is in a crab, all 28 wheels align to the runway heading.

I was in the left seat during the approach to Hill AFB when my dad asked me what type of approach I would like to fly. Wanting to fly this beast like a fighter jet , I responded that I would like to fly a 360-degree overhead traffic pattern to which he consented. I quickly discovered that after you put in the flight control inputs, you must wait several seconds for anything to happen. Conversely, fighters roll very rapidly to provide you the maneuverability that you need to defeat your adversary. The F-4 roll rate is 360 degrees per second. Later, when flying the Aggressor T-38, I enjoyed a 720 degrees per second roll rate. The Aggressor F-5E has 520 degrees per second roll rate but is much sturdier that the T-38. Once back in the air at Hill AFB on the way to Europe, the instructor told me the autopilot didn't work. He asked me if I wanted to hand-fly the airplane to Europe. I emphatically answered yes, because it was a challenge, and I always loved a challenge – still do! It sounded like fun. My father later asked me if I wanted to switch my career to fly transport aircraft. I thanked him, but said no.

There was no way I wanted to give up my dream for any reason.

Back at Udorn RTAFB, one day I was returning to base from a training mission, flying a straight-in approach at Udorn in my F-4 when I had a Boundary Layer Control (BLC) malfunction. This is a serious emergency in the F-4 because it affects your flight controls and could possibly start a fire in the aircraft. The emergency can be one of two types. For one type, you only have a few minutes, because the air can be hot and directed towards the fuel lines. The other type gives you more time before you lose control of the aircraft. The BLC warning light does not tell you which one it is. When this happened to me, I was on final of a straight-in approach at 700 ft. of altitude. The "zero-zero" feature of the (works at zero airspeed and zero altitude if the airplane is not moving) Martin Baker seat ejection envelope, due to the downward vector of a three-degree glide path, goes away at 300 ft. and is no longer zero-zero. My indications were a master caution light, BLC light, and almost all the caution lights on the telepanel flashing on and off. Also, the aircraft was doing sort of a "funky chicken," bobbing up and down slightly on the way to the runway. Deciding quickly, because I could still maintain reasonable aircraft control, I would fly it until it was no longer possible. I did make it to the end of the runway on approach speed and safely landed the aircraft. This was my first, but not last aircraft emergency, as there would be more!

At long last, the Air Force contacted me about my next assignment. They gave me a choice between ferrying one of the squadron F-4s to Royal Air Force (RAF) Lakenheath, in the United Kingdom (UK) taking a three-year assignment there in the F-4 or possibly being assigned to the 64th Fighter Weapons Squadron (Aggressors) at Nellis AFB, NV, flying the T-38A to simulate the Soviet Mig-21 (single-engine jet Soviet air-to-air fighter). This was a defining moment. The RAF Lakenheath assignment would keep me in the mainstream, a better career path for promotion. The Nellis Aggressor path would put me into an elite group, and I would only fly air-to-air missions. This would be more challenging and be better for my fighter pilot growth. Later down the road, at École Militaire (the French War College), the Superintendent, a lieutenant general, was astonished that I had arrived in Paris before classes started, found an apartment, and painted it without the help of the American Embassy. I responded, *"J'aime bien le challenge,"* which translated into English is, "I love a challenge." In this case, I chose the "challenge" option that made all the difference!

Chapter 4

Charter Member of Aggressors

I arrived at Nellis AFB on June 15, 1974, just twelve months after having arrived at Udorn RTAF. Again, I was greeted by heat. The heat in Thailand was a wet oppressive heat, whereas the heat in Las Vegas was a dry oppressive heat. A lot of my friends in Nevada and Arizona have always said, "oh it's a dry heat out here." The temperature that day was 115 degrees Fahrenheit, and the wind was blowing 35 mph, reminding me of a blast furnace. Until I could find a house, myself, my wife, and daughter stayed in a barracks for families at Indian Springs Auxiliary Airfield. We got some cooling at night from the noisy swamp coolers which dripped water in front of large fans. Of note was the fact that 115 degrees Fahrenheit on your lawn chair in the back yard translates to greater than 125 degrees Fahrenheit on the parking ramp for the aircraft on the flightline.

When I reported to the Deputy Commander for Operations for my assignment, I was overjoyed! I had been assigned to the Aggressor Squadron. Nothing but air-to-air! The squadron had been activated in 1972, so I just missed the cutoff for being a charter member in the 64th Fighter Weapons Squadron (FWS), later shortened to the 64th Aggressors. Happily, I became a charter member for the next two squadrons which were the 65th FWS (Aggressors) at Nellis AFB, and the 527th Tactical Fighter Training Aggressor Squadron (TFTAS) at RAF Alconbury, in the UK.

The Aggressor concept evolved from the "Red Baron" report, which was a summary of the lessons learned from the Vietnam Air War. Lieutenant Colonel Lloyd "Boots" Boothby is given the credit for the birth of the Aggressor Program, but Major Moody Suter was instrumental in pulling together the program. In addition, Major Suter drove the "Red Flag" concept through the Air Force chain of command. In the Korean War, the kill ratio against the enemy for air combat victories was known to be 10 enemy aircraft destroyed to 1 of ours (10 to 1). In Southeast Asia, the exchange ratio dropped to a very marginal number by the end of the war. There were many reasons.

The U.S. priority was given to bombs on target, carried by large strike force packages, using predictable flight paths going against sophisticated air defense networks. These networks included surface to air missiles, radar guided anti-aircraft fire, and modern enemy fighter aircraft controlled by ground radar. The enemy used Soviet style formations and tactics. The enemy aircraft were much smaller than ours. They could not be seen nose-on until less than a mile away. Air-to-air combat training before deploying to Southeast Asia consisted mostly of similar aircraft training (same type aircraft sparring against each other). It was limited to basic fighter maneuvers and one or two-ships against the same number and type of aircraft. Lieutenant Colonel Boothby and Major Suter pushed for a dedicated adversary, flying aircraft like the enemy's, using formation and tactics he used. Their pursuit was successful and the 64th FWS was activated within the 57th Fighter Weapons Wing on 15 October 1972. It was equipped at first with the highly maneuverable but hard to see T-38A Talons. They were painted with Soviet paint schemes and nose numbers to add to the realism. In April 1976, the Aggressors upgraded to the F-5E Tiger II when the buy for South Vietnam was no longer required because the war was over. The F-5E was a more realistic adversary and had gun camera film, which was useful for the debrief. In the T-38A and F-5E, each Aggressor pilot carried a tape recorder to record the airborne communications and personal commentary to facilitate the debrief.

The Aggressors trained their own. I was the second youngest pilot in the squadron and the training program was a big challenge for me! My best assets were energy and desire. We had Mig killers and even ex-Prisoners of War in our squadron, and our instructor pilots were the best. Most were senior captains. They were knowledgeable from the study of enemy tactics and assets that were made available to them. The upgrade training program consisted of learning not only the T-38A inside and out but knowing the enemy and his tactics. The flying portion started with the basics, one-on-one basic fighter maneuvers. To name just a few, there is lead pursuit, pure pursuit, and lag pursuit. You have the low-speed yo-yo, the high-speed yo-yo, and the barrel roll which is important for maintaining nose-tail position.

Once I started training F-4s in my adversarial role, my favorite maneuver was a huge barrel roll. When the F-4s broke (hard turn) into my aircraft over a mile out, I immediately went into the vertical, rolling and coming down the back side of the "egg," aligning fuselages and dropping into the heat missile weapon engagement zone (WEZ). The "egg" was the shape of the "g" envelope that included earth's gravity (narrow at the top and wide at the bottom). If your adversary gets behind you, guns defense is a last-ditch maneuver. Prior to that, hard breaks, idle power, and speed brakes could flush him out in front of you. I practiced those until they became second nature. You may have seen some of these maneuvers in Tom Cruise's top gun movies. That is what we did for a living, every day! The next step was air combat maneuvers, one against two and two-against two.

During this phase, formation and tactics began to come into play. We started to learn "military ruse and deception." I carried this concept forward when I returned to the Blue Forces (the U.S. and allied forces who would fight the enemy in time of conflict), in the F-15 Eagle at Bitburg AB in Germany, approaching the adversarial F-15s above 40,000 ft. of altitude so I would be above their radar coverage. As they passed below, I would swoop down on them, hopefully with the sun behind me, nose-on minimizing my cross-section. This earned me my Bitburg call sign of "Moonman" for coming in from so high into the fight (sometimes 45,000 ft. of altitude). Graduation day came when I flew in a fight of four white T-38s against four other white T-38s. Our airplanes were still white because we had not yet had them painted with Soviet camouflage paint schemes. I had to keep track of what eight aircraft who were near the center of the fight were doing all the time plus kill the adversaries and remain alive.

Ultimately, I achieved graduation and became a full-fledged Aggressor! Now I was ready to be assigned an academic topic to master. Each Aggressor pilot had a topic he would teach both locally and, on the road, when deployed to F-4 Blue Force bases in the United States' Tactical Air Command (TAC). My academic assignment was Soviet Fighter Formation and Tactics. I had 35 mm slides prepared, a script of notes, and carried my carousel with me on every deployment. The host unit would place it into their slide projector and display it on a screen allowing me to teach my academics.

I am standing in front of my F-5E getting ready for another big Red Flag mission. (Photographer unknown, Nellis AFB, NV, circa 1975)

Life as an Aggressor pilot was very challenging, but very rewarding and a ton of fun! Our job was to get the Blue Forces trained to kill us and for them not to get shot. If the reverse happened, we had more work to do. Our deployments to an F-4 base usually lasted two weeks. For a motivated unit, at the end of two weeks, the F-4 crews usually had made significant progress. We also supported the F-4 414th Fighter Weapons School locally at Nellis AFB, and the F-4

Instructor Course at Luke AFB, in Phoenix, AZ. This translated to being on the road 60 percent of the time.

We had some fun times off-duty occasionally also. One Christmas, all the families came down to the squadron. When we went out to the ramp, Captain Rich "Tuna" Hardy, dressed in a Santa Claus suit, taxied up to the group, bringing a sack of Christmas gifts for the kids. The kids then opened them up in the squadron building. One time at Luke AFB I got a glazed donut, put it on a stick, and opened the door on Tuna briefing his mission to give him the donut.

It was not unusual to fly twice a day when not flying Red Flag missions. Each flight entailed two to three full scale air-to-air engagements. Enroute to the area, we would perform ranging exercises, where we would close in on an F-4 two or four-ship formation nose on from greater than one mile out into 500 ft. This was so that the good guys could accustom their eyes to detecting a small cross-section fighter attacking their element or the other element in one mile line abreast formation. Once in the working area, the flights would split up and fly out of visual range from each other usually to opposite ends of the training area to set up for a head-on attack. Aggressors would use both ground-controlled radar and their own eyeballs to maneuver using adversary formations and tactics. The objective was to reach a firing position behind the F-4 formations to get a simulated "kill" shot. After the flight, the lead Aggressor pilot would orchestrate the debrief. He would draw the flight paths out on the blackboard with colored chalk, pointing out the good moves by the F-4s and areas for improvement. As Aggressors we had been specifically trained for this mission. We probably flew twice as often as the Blue Force pilots, but it was a critical part of our charter to remain humble. Our goal was to get the good guys trained to kill us bad guys. which was how we measured success!

Our deployments consisted mostly to operational F-4 units in the U.S., such as Seymour Johnson AFB or Eglin AFB, FL. I was primarily in a Luke-Seymour cycle prior to the launch of Red Flag, but I did snag an Eglin deployment one time. The units at Eglin AFB fought hard and optimized the flight envelopes of their aircraft. Located on the Florida coast, a short distance from the fully supersonic training areas in the Gulf of Mexico, they had maximum opportunity for realistic supersonic training.

A project in which I participated for the Aggressors was the investigation of the Air Combat Maneuvering Range (ACMR), at Miramar Naval Air Station (NAS) in San Diego, CA. The ACMR relied on pods being carried on the participating aircraft, allowing the exact flight path to be recorded for an accurate flight debrief. I represented the Aggressor

Community, and Captain Ron Keys (later General Ron Keys, TAC Commander) represented the 414th Fighter Weapons School. At Miramar NAS our goal was to see if there were any lessons learned from the Navy's ACMR that we could capture for the USAF Nellis AFB operation. For the U.S. Air Force (USAF), the implemented system was similar. It was named the Air Combat Maneuvering Instrumentation System, or ACMI. The USAF system was soon implemented and in place for Red Flag operations.

In October 1975, the 65th Fighter Weapons Squadron in which I was a charter member was formed out of members of the 64th Fighter Squadron. It started operations with the F-5E. I was fortunate enough to go to the factory at Palmdale, CA, pick up a brand-new F-5E, and fly it back to Nellis AFB. New aircraft smell is very similar to new car smell.

As my additional duty in the 65th, I served as the squadron commander's executive officer, overseeing his administrative duties. The 65th FWS building was adjacent to the 64th FWS building. The ACMI building and the 414th Fighter Weapons School buildings were nearby. It is no wonder that they call Nellis AFB the Home of the Fighter Pilot!

On November 29, 1975, thanks to Major Moody Suter, with the support of General Dixon, TAC Commander, Nellis AFB was the site of the first Red

Flag exercise. Red Flag is still alive today at Nellis and Eielson AFBs. This is still a large-scale exercise, simulating combat in a full-scale war as closely as possible. Major Suter advocated that the greatest loss to our combat air crews was in the first ten days of combat. In a two-week period, Red Flag gives us those first ten missions. The goal is for the United States to dominate combat operations when required. I had the good fortune to fly as an Aggressor, first in the T-38, then in the F-5E. I flew in the first six Red Flag exercises. Each Red Flag mission was a 12-hour day. The day started with arriving at the squadron at 6:00 a.m. in time to make a line-up card with all the members of your four-ship. Then you had to check weather and NOTAMS (Notices to Airmen). This was followed by attending a mass briefing with all Blue and Red Forces. Then you split up to get a mass Red Force brief, followed by your four-ship brief, then finally your two-ship element brief. The next step was pre-flight, take-off, and fly to your area of responsibility.

My favorite area to patrol was between the first two north-south ridge lines north of Nellis. This is where the uninitiated Blue Forces would turn ninety degrees to the left to proceed through what we called "student gap." (a large gap in the ridge line) in a highly predictable straight line to their target area. I flew at 100 ft. above ground level (AGL) at 400-450 knots of airspeed to avoid radar or visual detection. As the four-ships of Blue Forces flew through the student gap, I would sneak up behind them, one at a time, and get a simulated heat missile shot off. I worked my way up from Blue 4 up to the flight leader. As we carried ACMI pods, we could verify our "kills" as part of our debrief process.

When I was later an Aggressor at RAF Alconbury in the UK, the leaders at RAF Coltishall asked me if I could brief them on lessons learned from Red Flag as they were preparing for their upcoming Red Flag deployment. I agreed and the first major point we discussed was to pick varied routes to the target area and avoid student gap. I later learned that they had done quite well, having done their homework before their deployment!

Throughout the tactical air forces 5,000 ft. of altitude was the "hard deck" for training except at Red Flag. The Aggressors and Red Flag were built on the principle of train like you expect to fight. Consequently, one of the first things that I did when I joined the United States Air Forces in Europe (USAFE) was to design a training mission for the USAFE syllabus to step down the Blue Force Dissimilar Air Combat Training (DACT) safely to 100 ft. The Blue Forces in Europe deployed to Zaragoza, Spain for bombing and gunnery training. The weather was much better there compared to the UK and Central

Europe. There were also training areas there where this new low altitude training mission could be flown.

Back to Nellis AFB, after a Red Flag mission was flown, the process was reversed somewhat. First there was the mass debrief of Blue and Red Forces together. Then as Aggressors, we sought out and debriefed with Blue Forces that we had engaged. If possible, we would go to the ACMI debrief room, where the flight paths were depicted as they had been flown. There we conducted the debrief with your own forces if you had not operated as a single. We often split up to multiply our possible engagements with the Blue Forces. A single ship simulated a two-ship element. Later, as an F-15 Eagle pilot in the Dirty Dozen, we would go to the Philippines for Cope Thunder, flown out of Clark AB. This exercise was based on the same principle as Red Flag, but on a slightly smaller scale.

I also had the opportunity to participate in an F-5 flight manual conference at Edwards AFB. The flight manuals (commonly called Dash 1s) are continuously updated when significant discoveries are made that affect safety of flight or operation of the aircraft. Attending this conference, I was able to vote for my unit as to what would be included and how it would be said. It is very expensive for each page that must be changed because the information is published and distributed throughout the world to all the operators and maintainers of the aircraft.

I flew as often as I could much the same as I always have. On one occasion I had deployed for two back-to-back two-week deployments. This put me on the road for four straight weeks. We usually had off time on the weekends when we deployed, but our squadron needed volunteers for flying out the allotted hours on a weekend cross-country. That would be me! I distinctly remember one evening in the bar after flying all day on that Saturday, I came up with the brilliant idea for an Aggressor Top Gun double elimination BFM tournament. This was to see who the best pilot was (this was way before Tom Cruise thought about it for *Top Gun - 1986*). We planned it out on a cocktail napkin. When I took the idea back to Nellis to the operations officer, for obvious reasons it didn't "fly."

As an Aggressor at Nellis AFB, I only experienced two aircraft problems. This was while flying the T-38 which was designed as a trainer, not a fighter. The first one occurred just after takeoff on the climb-out. All at once I had runaway elevator trim. I pulled out the circuit breaker to no avail. It took nearly all my strength to hold the stick forward to keep the aircraft from a severe pitch up and stall (not enough air flowing over the wing to sustain flight) with loss of control of the aircraft. At that time, we all carried a paperback book in the cockpit called the Enroute Supplement. This contained data on all the airports in the United States where you could land an aircraft. I stuck my Enroute Supplement between my ejection seat pan and the control stick to relieve the pressure. Then I declared an emergency and turned back to base. I slowed down, lowered the landing gear, and checked to see if I could maintain aircraft control at landing speed. The good news was that there was less of an issue at approach speed. I landed the aircraft safely and gave it back to the maintainers to fix the problem.

My other aircraft issue was on a cross-country flight when I had planned to stop for fuel at Reese AFB, at Lubbock, TX. I thought it would be a good base to service the airplane, because it was equipped with T-38s. The forecast weather was good, but upon arrival at Reese AFB (closed in 1997) I was faced with a 35-knot crosswind with an aircraft limit of 25 knots. Unable to proceed to any other airport due to fuel remaining, I planned to land as far as possible on the runway upwind, which I did. With all the flight controls available to me (rudder and aileron), I was able to keep the aircraft under control. It drifted to the downwind side of the runway as I slowed it down to taxi speed. Upon postflight inspection, I had worn one of the tires down to the white cord. As Reese AFB was a T-38 base, they had plenty of new tires. After a quick tire change, I was on my way. I did have two pilot issues while flying at Nellis. The first one was when I was flying in the back seat of a pilot who was getting his required minimum hours for pay. He was completely qualified in the T-38, but he was not an Aggressor pilot. He decided to proceed northwest of the base, then he dropped down to low altitude and flew at a high speed. He didn't have it mapped out and our altitude was too low to pick up the electronic navigation signal from Nellis AFB which would have given us bearing and range to the field. Our speed was up, and our fuel was burning fuel at a rapid rate. It would have been very embarrassing to have had to eject for a double-engine flameout. Finally, I asked him if he knew our range and bearing back to Nellis. Since he didn't know, I asked him to zoom up to 20,000 ft. of altitude to get that information. He did and we discovered that we had just enough fuel to get back home safely. It was a little tense, but not as bad as the poor F-106 pilot on a Red Flag mission who flamed out after landing. He was taxiing back to parking, but he didn't quite make it to the chocks.

The second issue was when another pilot and I were flying on a cross-country navigation flight to a base in California. As it turned out, the other pilot's grandmother lived along our planned route of flight. He wanted to do a flyover of her ranch so she would be impressed with the fact that he was an Air Force fighter pilot. I didn't stop him, but I held back circling a few miles away until he rejoined the formation. I do not believe we had been reported for a possible deviation, because I never heard another word about it.

After two years as a Nellis Aggressor pilot, TAC reasoned that a similar program in Europe would be a good idea. To ensure a successful launch, 25 percent of the United States Air Forces in Europe (USAFE) Aggressor Squadron pilots had to come from Nellis AFB. The commander told us that we could either volunteer for RAF Alconbury or at the end of our three-year tour at Nellis AFB expect a non-fighter follow-on assignment. This was another point where a choice would define my destiny. It seemed that the best fighter assignments were often outside the United States. I, of course, was one of the first volunteers! My second child, Scott III, born in Las Vegas, my wife and daughter would get to go on my second overseas tour. My 1973 Buick Le Sabre Luxus, which I had purchased while still in Thailand on a ten percent discount program could not navigate the narrow streets in rural English towns. That was not going to fly, so it stayed in the United States and my brother Larry sold it for me. Instead, I shipped my orange 1964 Volkswagen Beetle giving me a much more fuel-efficient vehicle small enough to fit into the English trajectory. The Brits affectionally called our larger vehicles "Yank Tanks."

My arrival at RAF Alconbury, in the United Kingdom (UK) was to the hottest summer in 350 years. The heat seemed to follow me! I joined the Royal Air Force (RAF) Mess (Officers Club). I found they had relaxed the requirement for ties for men. The public houses (pubs) all ran out of lager beer, cooler than the stout beer, which is always served at room temperature. The lack of rain from June through August contributed to a haze layer that rose above the island that gradually rose to 10,000 ft. above ground level until the rains resumed in September. RAF Alconbury is in East Anglia located about 60 miles north of London. During the three years I lived there, I found there were on average two weeks of sunshine each May and two weeks of sunshine each September. As far as flying was concerned, RAF Alconbury and Hahn AB, in Germany, tied for the poorest flying weather anywhere in the world. Takeoffs, initial climbs, and approaches were almost always in clouds. Normally, once you were above 5-6,000 ft. you were in clear skies which was good because that is where we trained. Our home training area was in the Wash Air Training Area (ATA), a supersonic-capable airspace between the coasts of East Anglia and Lincolnshire.

The initial cadre for the 527th TFTAS on the RAF Alconbury F-5E *flightline. (Base Photographer, RAF Alconbury, UK, circa 1976)*

In June 1976, as a charter member of the 527th TFTAS, our airplanes were just starting to arrive. A brilliant lieutenant at Kelly AFB in San Antonio, TX came up with the great idea that if you removed the wings of the F-5E, you could fit eight of the birds into a C-5. This negated the need to fly them one at a time island hopping to their intended base of employment. As an additional duty, I checked out as a Functional Check Flight (FCF) pilot at RAF Alconbury, as I had done at Nellis AFB. FCFs were performed on the F-5E when major maintenance was done before they were returned to normal operations. This included maintenance such as changing an engine or in our case putting the wings back on the airplane.

My first aircraft issue in Europe happened on my first FCF. One Saturday morning, when I started my airplane up for an FCF, I got smoke in the cockpit coming through the air conditioning vents. In my mind, where there was smoke there was fire. I called the tower, shut down the engine, and egressed from the airplane. Soon thereafter my commander Lieutenant Colonel "Big Fella" Bruce MacLennan told me it was a non-issue. The engines were packed in cosmoline, and it burned off the first time the engines were started. It would have been nice to know that before starting up!

I had my second aircraft issue while flying the F-5E in Europe that was not life-threatening, but a little aggravating. Part of the preflight was to test both fire detection circuits. The fire detection loop would let you know if you had a possible fire situation in either or both engines. This would allow you to shut down the affected engine and fly back to base on the other engine. I was at Zaragosa AB, Spain ready to fly back to RAF Alconbury when I tested the fire loop. On startup and pre-takeoff checks, the right engine fire loop test failed. I called the operations officer, Major C.T. Wang. He stated he would get the part sent down. After five days the part came, but it was for the left engine and the parts were not interchangeable. I was not a happy camper! I was not flying, and I was burning a lot of daylight (one of General Ron Fogleman's favorite expressions). In my frustration, I asked the ops officer if I could fly back commercial and return to get the airplane when it was fixed. I guess that was a bridge too far! I was ordered to remain with the airplane. Three days later the correct fire loop arrived. It was installed and the boat tail was replaced. I then proceeded to fly the airplane back to RAF Alconbury.

Murphy's Law applied when the wrong fire loop was sent to me for installation. (Photographer unknown, Zaragosa AB, SP, circa 1978)

My third aircraft issue while assigned to RAF Alconbury happened when I was supporting the Ramstein AB Air Show as a static display pilot with our squadron commander, Big Fella. On the big day, he said he would take the first half of the day and I would take the second half. He was no fool! It was a day for record crowds and record heat. I stood by my F-5E all through the heat of the afternoon answering questions about the airplane and our mission. By 5:00 p.m., the show was over, and crowds were dissipating. I elected to head for the Officers Club believing all would be well since the aircraft was roped off. When I arrived the next morning to fly my airplane back to RAF Alconbury, it was not flyable. I discovered that one of the oil caps had disappeared and the pitot tube in front of the nose of the aircraft had been bent straight up at a 90-degree angle.

I knew I had to wait for the oil cap to come over from Alconbury because there were not any F-5s based in Germany, but a new pitot tube would be depot level maintenance. I found the pitot tube was very malleable, making it easy to just straighten it out. The pitot tube was part of the system to provide airspeed in the cockpit which was calculated by measuring the difference between ram air (air coming to the front of the aircraft) and static air (air at the side of the aircraft). I calculated the speed from my checklist that I should reach after accelerating to the first 1,000 ft. marker and reasoned if the airspeed was correct at that point, then the airplane was "fixed." On my takeoff roll, the airspeed was right on the money at the 1,000 ft. marker allowing me to return home with the airplane.

My primary duty as in the U.S. was to train Blue Forces in how to kill me and not get killed themselves. Weather was a challenge compared to the United States. The ceilings and visibilities were much lower, on average, compared to the United States. Also, with the cloud tops rising to 5,000 to 10,000 ft. of altitude on a regular basis, routinely the air-to-air engagements were fought without reference to the ground. We had the Wash ATA supersonic range, where we trained units based in the UK. This included units that flew into RAF Alconbury, such as the Bitburg F-15s.

We deployed to RAF Bentwaters to fly Dissimilar Air Combat Training (DACT) against their F-4s or those of RAF Woodbridge, as the two bases were near each other. The F-4s from RAF Leuchars, Scotland flew into Alconbury for training as did the Jaguars of RAF Coltishall. Here's when preparing the Jaguar pilots for Red Flag that was previously addressed occurred. Sometimes impromptu visual lookout engagements occurred in Europe. One day after an FCF I had sufficient fuel remaining to update my low altitude high speed flying skills out in the Wash area. I dropped down to 100 ft. of altitude, accelerating to 450 knots (517 mph). Shortly thereafter, when checking "6" I discovered I had been "tapped" (snuck up behind) by an RAF Buccaneer. At RAF Alconbury, we had the Russian bear on our patch. There's a saying that "Sometimes you get the bear and sometimes the bear gets you." That day the bear got me!

My deployment rate remained at 60 percent, deploying from Denmark in the north to Iran in the

Middle East. When flying against U.S. forces in Central Europe, we trained in areas called TRAs, short for training areas. The TRAs were close to bases where we deployed, such as Hahn AB, Zweibruchen AB, Spangdahlem AB, Bitburg AB, or Ramstein AB.

The disadvantage of the TRAs was that they were limited to subsonic flying. It was difficult but necessary to stay subsonic in a full-up dogfight over land in Germany. We also deployed to Camp New Amsterdam (CNA), the location of Soesterberg AB, in The Netherlands. During that deployment, we could fight supersonic out over the North Sea which allowed employing our aircraft to their full capabilities. The deployment to Soesterberg was a joy. They had enviable stability in their ranks, meaning their pilots stayed in the squadron long enough to achieve a high degree of proficiency. Like Eglin AFB in TAC, their pilots trained exclusively in unrestricted airspace under full supersonic conditions. During the entire one-week deployment there, I flew with a head cold. I was able to overcome it during the air-to-air engagements and my ears cleared readily throughout all the rapid altitude changes. Upon redeploying from the Soesterberg trip, I got an ear block after I made an afterburner climb up to my cruise altitude of 35,000 ft.

I was a Charter Member of the 527th TFTAS at RAF Alconbury, UK. (Photographer unknown, RAF Alconbury, UK, circa 1976)

Upon the descent, I found I couldn't clear my ears. I didn't follow the correct procedure of levelling off or climbing until my ears were cleared. Not wanting to wait until I became incapacitated in a single-seat airplane, I continued the descent to landing. I immediately went to the flight surgeon in great pain, where he pierced my eardrum to relieve the pressure. This translated to three weeks on the ground until my eardrum healed. Once again, *Pretty Woman - 1990*, "Big Mistake ..Huge!"

On a deployment to Ramstein AB, I had a couple of interesting experiences. The first one was during an engagement with an F-4E piloted by an individual who had been the back seater (WSO) of a Vietnam War Ace from the 555th TFS Triple Nickel and shot down five Migs. This WSO's reward was to go to UPT, and he ultimately ended up in the F-4 front seat. During our slow speed maneuvering engagement, I was able to get a guns tracking solution on his aircraft. During the debrief he asked me how I could have done that because he had done a hammerhead stall. This is where you blend in top aileron and bottom rudder to swap ends of the airplane. This allows you to convert rapidly from nose high to nose low. I replied simply that I had done a hammerhead stall to the inside of his hammerhead stall. Trying hard to stay humble!

The other interesting flight at Ramstein AB was the day we flew in a close-by TRA, flying against the Ramstein F-4s. The weather was forecast to be good, allowing visual recoveries. Unexpectedly, we got a radio call from our duty officer at squadron operations to return immediately, because the weather was going south rapidly. There were several F-4s and F5s that had to be recovered by Ramstein Approach Control using instrument approaches, one at a time. I got in the queue and got vectored onto a 25-mile downwind. I was starting to get low on fuel and saw some holes in the clouds, convincing me to cancel my clearance and I started to fly directly to the field. Not cooperating, the clouds started closing in and I had to go back to Approach Control for an instrument approach. I declared minimum fuel (just enough to safely proceed to the field and land with no delays) and made it back without having to declare emergency fuel. I was glad to be back on the ground after that recovery! I did not flame out taxiing back like the poor F-106 pilot in Red Flag, but I had little fuel to spare.

Every two years, North Atlantic Treaty Organization (NATO) conducted a large-scale exercise called Oksbol, off the coast of Denmark. It was a sad day when one of our pilots fatally flew into the North Sea. In the six fighter squadrons I was in, only the first and last didn't lose a pilot. Some of that is luck, a small percentage is aircraft malfunctions, but I believe most of it is in how you fly and how you lead your pilots if you are in a leadership position. In the 13th TFS Panther Pack at Udorn RTAF all of us were deployed overseas, partly in combat and partly in training to go back into combat. We had focus and minimum family distractions. We had been discouraged from bringing our wives to live near the base, for their safety. I believe this helped both pilots and maintainers in keeping our focus. My last fighter squadron was the 12th TFS Dirty Dozen at Kadena AB, Japan. I was the Operations Officer responsible for the combat skills and safety of my pilots. I let EVERYONE know up front that WE WERE GOING TO FLY: HARD, right up to the LIMITS of the aircraft and ourselves but not beyond, and by the RULES. I also said that we would be the best! There will be more on that later.

A project in which I was able to participate as a USAFE Aggressor was the 1979 bed down of the ACMI range at Decimomannu AB, a U.S. base in Sardinia, off the west coast of Italy. The ACMI range offered USAFE fighter forces the opportunity for supersonic DACT training. This was not possible over land in Central Europe. The weather was also more suitable for unrestricted operations unless the winds were too high for potential sea rescue. My part of the project involved spending a week in the new ACMI van recently fabricated. I was to coordinate with the contractor of the system. This was to be done prior to arrival and operation of USAFE aircraft. Because I had participated in the installation of the ACMI at Nellis AFB, I had a point of reference for this project. It was interesting because the quarters at Decimomannu AB had no hot water, making cold showers the staple for seven days. It was a critical initiative for USAFE DACT training as I would deploy there an F-15 pilot many times in the future.

RAF Farnborough, UK was the site of a big air show every year with many demonstrations, static displays, and flyovers. I had the distinct honor of being the F-5E flyover pilot one year, which entailed proceeding to a holding point away from the show and leaving at a prescribed time and speed to fly by the crowd. The UK appreciated our F-5Es' contribution to their defense. I also had a temporary duty assignment (TDY) to Iran, which was quite an experience. Another Aggressor pilot, Captain Roy Stuckey and I were assigned to train the Iranian Air Force pilots flying the

F-5E and F-5F at Shiraz AB, Iran. Roy and I flew in the back seats of their F-5Fs, and it was as interesting as it sounded. The Iranians put us up in a hotel and we had to ride a bus to the base each morning. Shortly after the call to worship each day (nothing moved during the call to worship), we departed the hotel. The bus ride was an experience to say the least! The driver was either applying full throttle or full brakes. Somehow, we made it to and from the hotel without incident. One day we had to wait until the afternoon to go to work because everyone in the country was prohibited from moving around while they took the national census.

Meanwhile, my body was not compatible with the local beer. I had to run for the toilet just before and just after each sortie. At the hotel, we had western style toilets but, on the base, we had two pads for our feet with a hole in the floor between the foot pads. We called it the "Norden bombsight." You had to be very careful to avoid "shacking" your flight suit. My adverse condition persisted until two days after returning to England. Shiraz had squadrons of F-4Es, F-5E/Fs, and F-14s (Navy Tomcat two-engine jet fighter and long range interceptor). The nephew of the Shah of Iran was slated to go to the U.S. UPT course. Failure was not an option, resulting in the nephew receiving a checkout in all three airplanes before his departure. What was amazing was that a motorcycle motorcade escorted him from where he parked his airplane to the squadron building for the debrief.

The Iranians even had an aerial demonstration team which mirrored the maneuvers of the USAF Thunderbirds. They did this in addition to their normal fighter pilot duties. I flew with a few of these pilots, and they were reasonably proficient. On one flight, I was in the back seat of one young pilot who lost his heading indicator inflight and didn't know how to get back to the base. I gave this new pilot a simulated no-gyro ground-controlled approach (GCA), and initially called for him to "Start turn." When the nose of his airplane was pointed at the base, I called for him to "Stop turn." What could have been a fuel exhaustion and ejection situation had he been alone ended up as an uneventful recovery. The off duty highlight of the trip was a visit to the Persepolis, which was only 30 miles from Shiraz. The Persepolis was built by Darius in the sixth century B.C. and the burial site of Cyrus II. Alexander the Great burned it to the ground in 330 B.C. The ruins were amazing as was seeing all that history!

Resuming duties at RAF Alconbury as an instructor pilot, I was responsible for checking out new pilots in the local area. Because we only had the single seat F-5Es, I was in a different airplane, flying the "chase" position. This consisted of flight slightly aft of the "wing" position (putting your wingtip light in the star of the lead aircraft) maintaining wingtip clearance and remaining lower on the other aircraft. Flying chase was even more demanding than refueling on the tanker. If you were too far forward, you could get hit if the other aircraft broke into you. If you were too far aft, you could get "slung out" and be left in the dust if he turned away from you. The trickiest maneuver to follow was when the forward aircraft did his 60-degree bank turn "break" from initial to downwind in the traffic pattern. You had to start your turn near simultaneously and add power to fly a circle slightly larger than his and not fall behind. Compared to that, landing my Mooney in a 25-knot crosswind is a walk in the park.

The flying at RAF Alconbury was good if you had the weather to fly. In the military, you need landing minimums to takeoff. Mine were as low as possible, meaning we had to be really "socked in" to keep me on the ground. It did happen though. One two-week period the command inspection team was on base to conduct an ORI for the RF-4 squadron and we didn't turn a wheel (fly) for two weeks. During those no-fly days, it was into the vault which was at least ten degrees colder than outside of the vault. On those days I not only wore long johns, but a turtleneck under my Nomex flight suit and even put on my flight jacket. Once inside we would study and beef up our academic briefings. We presented these briefings not only to USAFE crews, but to (NATO) crews.

While at RAF Alconbury, my second son Matt was born. The hospital at RAF Lakenheath where he was born was over an hour away. At 10:00 p.m. I put Patty in the back seat of our 1965 Mark II Jaguar and put the pedal to the metal. Good thing the Jag would do better than 100 mph, because there was no guarantee he wouldn't have been born enroute! As this was her third child, she expected to have a quick delivery, but Matt wasn't born until the next morning, defying conventional wisdom. I returned home to take care of my other two children. When I returned to RAF Lakenheath in civilian clothes at a reasonable speed the next day to retrieve my family, the base was having a training exercise. They were not going to let me into the hospital because I was not wearing a gas mask. I finally convinced the guard at the entrance that I was on leave, from RAF Alconbury, and exempted from the exercise. I had to sign a roster declaring I was not participating before I could get my family.

I would often volunteer for cross-country flights to get additional flying. This was to help the squadron fly out its allocated flying hours and to have fun. Like the 64th Aggressors at Nellis, if you didn't fly out your hours for the year, you got fewer flying hours the next year. For this flight, the maintainers hung three external fuel tanks on my airplane to maximize the flying time. Needing somewhere to go that was not close by, I flew to Torrejon AB in Spain, landed, and refueled, then flew to Aviano AB, Italy. The next morning, I flew back to the UK. I called ahead for fuel, minimizing my time on the ground.

A totally more interesting cross-country was planned for Copenhagen, Denmark, where I went with another pilot in the squadron, because it was better to fly as a two-ship for mutual support. My job was to file the flight plans and fill out the navigation logs. His job was to check the NOTAMS and make sure we could comply. We took off on a Friday and headed for Copenhagen, only to be told by ATC when we entered Danish air space that we didn't have clearance for Copenhagen. We didn't want to return to RAF Alconbury, so we asked for a clearance to Aalborg AB. We knew the nearby town to Aalborg would keep us busy until we flew home, because we knew it from our Oksbol exercises.

We found a hotel room that we could afford that was small enough that you had to go outside to change your mind, but it would suffice as a place to crash. We proceeded to check out expensive Danish beer and had a great time. In fact, we found everyone very friendly, and our new friends even invited us to a party that Sunday night in Sweden! Wonder what that would have been like? The plan was for the entire group that we had been hanging out with in Aalborg to all meet at the ferry Sunday afternoon. We called back to Major C.T. Wang, the operations officer, to see if we could keep the planes an extra day. Much to our chagrin, we had to fly home Sunday because the planes were needed for the local flying schedule back at RAF Alconbury on Monday.

At the three-year point, I knew my tour at RAF Alconbury would be ending soon and I reasoned that I might be able to get support to stay in the command and maybe even upgrade to the F-15 Eagle. This was another defining moment! I was proficient as a fighter pilot, but I could not be an Aggressor forever. I signed up for a cross-country flight to Bitburg AB. I had coordinated with the Assistant Deputy Commander of Operations (ADO) of the 36th TFW to meet with him on a Saturday morning. I flew in the night before, and the weather was bad enough to cause me to land at bare minimums! There was a cloud just before mid-field that was blocking a clear view of the departure end of the runway. After I landed, I remained on the centerline, slowing down as I went into the cloud. I managed to come out of the cloud, still on the centerline. I was met by the Supervisor of Flying (SOF), who was amazed. He said, "I don't know how you did that, but you are here!"

I spent the night at the BOQ and proceeded to meet with the ADO the next morning. After a brief introduction, I came right to the point and said, "Sir, how would you like to hire an ex-Aggressor?" He indicated he would check it out, and soon after returning to Alconbury I got my orders for the 53rd TFS, the Tiger Squadron at Bitburg. Shortly following the orders, I got a call from Lieutenant Colonel Tom Goldman, the 53rd TFS Squadron Commander, asking if I wanted to be a flight commander. Jumping with joy, I said, "Yes, that would be great!"

After the first 527th TFTAS DACT mission with the 401st TFW of Torrejón Air Base, SP in USAFE. From left to right: Captain Jim Kennedy, Captain Randy Royce, me, and Lieutenant Colonel "Big Fella" MacLennan. (Photographer unknown, RAF Alconbury, UK, Sep 16, 1976)

Chapter 5

Blue Force in the F-15 Eagle

Getting to Bitburg AB to fly the F-15 Eagle was an adventure. I sold my Jaguar to a German fighter pilot on exchange in the UK. His wife wanted a small station wagon for the family, but he wanted a sporty sedan. I hope he did not get into too much trouble for his need for speed. I had also sold my orange Volkswagen and bought a slightly larger higher performance green Volkswagen sedan. We had recently gone on vacation to Devon and Cornwall in our "new" Volkswagen. It was an interesting trip, with only three of the four cylinders working in the car and we had to leave the farmhouse early in Devon that we had rented, because their sheep came down with meningitis. No refund, but we didn't have to pay for the days we missed.

I checked into the 53rd TFS and they gave me a few days to find a place to settle my family before my checkout program would start. The base housing office told me I would have to wait at least six months to get on-base housing. This meant I would have to find something on the "Economy" (slang for off-base). After looking around for a couple of days, we found a nice house large enough for a family of five on top of a hill and on the low-level flight path for the German Air Force F-104s. This provided us an occasional reminder that our pilots were contributing to the defense of Western Europe. It was being rented out by the owner of the *Gasthaus* (guesthouse) in Wißmannsdorf with a beautiful setting.

Settled in, I reported to the squadron. I received my new patches for the wing, squadron, and "Eagle driver (F15 pilot)." I already had the command patch for USAFE. I also got my Tiger squadron scarf which was a part of my uniform whenever I was not flying. Then my training officer told me I was going to get a "local" checkout, which was what the DO at Homestead AFB had tried unsuccessfully to do for me in the F-4. I heard later that I got the very last one and everyone after me had to go through a formal course in the U.S. For my program, I was pointed to a storage cabinet and told that it contained the 35mm slide carousels for my academic training. I was also given a stack of manuals and regulations to include the aircraft flight manual (Dash 1), weapons system manual (Dash 34-1-1), USAFE Regulations with 36th TFW and 53rd TFS supplements. There was a saying that the weight of the manuals had to equal the weight of the airplane. In this case, it came close. The F-15 was a lot more complicated than an F-5. The Dash 1 gave instructions on how to fly the airplane. The Dash 34-1-1 was all about employing the F-15 as a weapon system. Both aircraft manuals and organizational regulations were updated on a regular basis. Before each flight, you had to see if there were any changes to incorporate into your "pubs" before you could fly. In addition to full size publications, you had the G-suit pocket size aircraft and weapons manual checklists, as well as an Inflight Guide. The Inflight Guide provided key information relevant to flying in and around Bitburg AB. In addition, whenever we flew, we carried all the instrument flight rules publications necessary for the intended area of operations. This included departure procedures, approach plates, and the Enroute Supplement.

The academic phase was completed prior to the beginning of the flight phase and only took a week, mostly because I was eager to fly the Eagle. I also took the instrument written, which was required once a year. At the beginning of the flight phase, all flights were conducted in the F-15B, which had a rear seat for the instructor, allowing him to give advice and ensure safe landings. I later checked out as an instructor pilot in the F-15. I can assure you that landing from the back seat is a real challenge! To successfully land from the back seat, you must fly a 180-degree tight pattern from the downwind leg rolling out the bank until just before you touch down on the runway. That is because you cannot see anything in front of you when you fly from the back seat. Once rolled out on final, you put an equal amount of grass on each side of the airplane. Then you know you are on the centerline of the runway. Once you have touched down, you can put an equal amount of asphalt on each side. Then you know you are staying on the runway.

The F-15 is a low wing loaded (a lot of wing surface for lift compared to the weight of the aircraft) airplane and lands much like the Cessna 172 (a GA high wing, four-seat, single-engine light aircraft). Like the Cessna, landing distance can be shortened by "aerobraking," which is holding the nose up after touching down, allowing aerodynamic drag to slow down. With a nice long runway and a touchdown close to the approach end, you could shine your rear end (show off), by slipping in a little power to keep the nose up high in the air until just before the last turnoff from the runway. I only did that once when I was in a feisty mood! With my F-4 air-to-air training for air combat and my five years as an Aggressor, my F-15 BFM and ACM upgrade training came easily. The new skill to learn was doing all this while operating the high-performance radar. The key elements were detection, target assignment, and approach to the firing envelope or weapons engagement zone (WEZ). This was an area for constant study and practice because there was a group of fighter pilots at Nellis AFB who continuously invented improvements for the radar and passed them on to industry to incorporate into the aircraft.

I was flying the F-15 Eagle at Bitburg AB, GE and commanding the C Flight of the 53rd TFS. (Photographer at 53rd TFS, Bitburg AB, GE, circa 1982)

Soon after checking out in the airplane my parents came for a visit. It was a chance for them to see their grandchildren and see the F-15 operations at Bitburg. This was an opportune time for the visit because they were there when we had an open day for families at the squadron. My mother got a high-speed F-15 taxi ride down the runway. I had coordinated for a back seat ride for my father, as he was still on active duty flying status and after all, he got me flights in his C-141 and C-5 at Travis AFB, CA.

My father got his F-15 flight at Bitburg AB, GE. (Photographer unknown, Bitburg AB, GE, circa 1980)

The wing commander was accommodating but the stipulation was that he could be in the same flight, but he had to be in a different aircraft. Before the flight my dad ate two chili cheese dogs in the snack bar. You guessed it ..they later ended up in his helmet bag! He appreciated the flight, as he had been destined for the P-51 in the Pacific Theater. This would have followed 35 combat missions in the B-24 in the European Theater during WWII, but his orders were cancelled because of Victory in Japan Day (V-J Day).

Chapter 6

Supporting the Cold War—F-15 DCA

Once mission-ready in the airplane, I flew as often as possible. I had a strong belief that a high level of proficiency was key to being effective if we entered combat and served as a life insurance policy. Even today, I am not getting ready for combat, but I fly over 200 hours per year to keep up my proficiency. Some of the techniques I used to get extra flying included coming into the squadron early in the morning when the weather was bad because I had the lowest possible weather minimums due to my experience level. When pilots with higher minimums had to come off the schedule due to bad weather, I would be standing at the duty desk ready to be added to the line-up. When each pilot was limited to eight sorties per month, I would try to get my eight as early in the month as possible positioning me in the latter part of the month to fill gaps in the schedule when other pilots were not available or qualified. I also checked out as an instructor as soon as possible because instructors flew more often. Lastly, I would listen up on the radio frequency to hear if a KC-135 or KC-10 tanker was in the vicinity. When that occurred, I would fly the planned mission in the TRA, go to the tanker to "snivel" extra gas, then return to the TRA to re-fly the planned mission. This didn't last forever because the operations officer believed this was too hard for the less experienced pilots. We learned from Vietnam that you fight like you train, and I believed I was getting my wingmen ready for combat.

Finally, the cross-country was an opportunity to get additional training and flying time. My ultimate cross-country as C Flight Commander was a weekend when we took off as a four-ship flight from Bitburg AB. We started out by first flying against the RAF Alconbury F-5E Aggressors in the Wash ATA. After engaging the F-5Es we landed at RAF Alconbury, debriefed, took off, flew against the Yeovilton AV-8B Harriers (a small jet fighter with vectored thrust) of the Royal Navy (RN), and recovered into RAF Lakenheath to spend the night. The following day we flew to Spain, "sniveling" some gas from a tanker at 16,000 ft. of altitude that was refueling some A-10s. Next, we flew an intercept mission against two Aggressor F-5Es in one of the Zaragosa AB training areas recovering into Torrejon AB. We could not fly DACT with them because we had not briefed it. Then we refueled on the ground there and took off for Aviano AB, in northern Italy. Almost on initial with a four-ship flight of F-15s, I got a lightning strike on my nose cone. The only physical evidence of damage was a small burn spot, but the massively bright flash on my windscreen temporarily blinded me for a few seconds. To get into Aviano AB, I had obtained a Prior Permission Required (PPR) number from Base Operations.

Upon landing, the DO met us, accusing me of "arm wrestling" his airman to get the number. He had activity at Aviano AB that he wanted to keep discreet, which caused him to give us two hours' notice to get off the field. I called the Bitburg AB Command Post to let them know about our change in itinerary and we flew home missing an overnight stay in Aviano. We also missed an intercept mission with four Canadian F-104s out of Sollingen AB, GE the next morning. All in all, we had a great time, hitting most of Central Europe and getting some excellent DACT. After the cross-country, we found out that we had been turned in for sniveling gas and that the new squadron policy was no more refueling unless it was officially on the schedule. This goes back to Rule #1: *If you don't file a flight plan, you can't get a clearance*; i.e., if we had not tried for extra gas, we would have never received any. It had worked for some time before getting the restriction. A key role we served at Bitburg AB was that of air defense alert. In keeping with the defensive mission of NATO, air defense alert, along with counterair assumed that the USAFE forces stayed on their side of the border, defending the territory of the NATO nations. On alert, a quick response was required. To stay in peak condition, we would often get practice scrambles. This necessitated sliding down a pole from the second floor of the alert barn, quickly climbing up the ladder to get in our airplanes, starting the engines, and taking off in minimum time. We took off in full afterburner and quickly climbed to cruise altitude, then be notified if it was a real or practice scramble. If it was a practice scramble, we would often climb to over 30,000 ft. of altitude, where we practiced supersonic intercepts. For holiday planning, married pilots often took alert on New Year's Eve, while bachelor pilots sat alert on Christmas, allowing the married pilots to be with their families. It was a system that worked well for morale. Sitting alert was an ideal opportunity to work on your master's degree, and I subscribed to the plan, finishing mine in International Relations from Troy State University. The new rule of thumb was that you needed that to progress beyond captain. Enrolling in an extension master's program also reduced the number of times you had to sit in the tower at night as the Supervisor of Flying (SOF).

In the middle of my tour, I was "invited" by my father to attend his retirement ceremony at Scott AFB, IL. I would have preferred to remain flying at Bitburg, but a higher calling took me and my wife back for the ceremony. It was a beautiful event with sunshine, a parade, and a nice reception, culminating a 40-year career for my father, whose last assignment was Air

Rescue Commander, retiring as a major general. This assignment was complete with Jolly Green footprints leading up to his residence in base quarters. The most dramatic event of the retirement trip was when my brother, Larry, a career Army military policeman who retired as a colonel, took out his temporary dental bridge and placed it on the bar and downing a flaming tequila.

Most of our training at home base consisted of two versus two similar ACM in the TRAs. This was good for radar work, even though our true adversaries would have been more difficult to acquire, but the approach to a merge was limited to subsonic speed. Once the turning combat started, ACM meant fighting an airplane with the same capabilities. That was the difference between similar and dissimilar training. We used to call it like "kissing your sister." Compare that with flying against an airplane with vectored thrust or a delta wing for example.

Our best training came flying DACT, either with another NATO fighter or with the Aggressors. For other training, we deployed to RAF Alconbury to fight with supersonic long-range setups in the Wash ATA and participated in joint exercises or deployments within NATO. One of these types of exercises was Anorak Express. Our Bitburg F-15s were based at Bodø, Norway, north of the Artic circle. This brought a new meaning to the word cold. You had to shave the night before you flew or else your face would freeze when you went out into the cold the next morning. We had to wear arctic parkas while flying we flew and heavy mukluk boots instead of our normal leather boots. Immersion "Poopy" suits were required under our "g" suits, for warmth and additional hours of survivability if you had to eject. Although, with the frigid water temperatures of Norway, the suits would have only given an extra matter of minutes survival time. When we took off without afterburner in "military," or full throttle power, the aircraft literally leapt into the air, at half the takeoff distance back at Bitburg.

Our mission there included escort, intercept, and some DACT. The Norwegian F-104 squadron pilots were excellent hosts. I was afforded the unique opportunity of a back seat F-104 ride. From there I could see the sides of the mountains while flying through the fjords at 400 knots by looking out the top of the canopy at what seemed like only a few feet away. My pilot took terrain masking to a new level. On the recovery, he let me fly the pattern from the back seat but cautioned me not to get slow. I did get a couple of knots slow, and the pedal shaker came on, causing my front-seater to take back the airplane. The F-104 has very small wings, and even two knots too slow and could lead to a stall.

An interesting deployment was to Eskisehir AB, Turkey, where we flew against their F-4Es, with smokeless engines. I was the deployment project officer, and I planned the deployment, redeployment, and supervised the day-to-day operations. The flying was productive, and the Turkish pilots challenged us in the air-to-air arena. We also had a chance to learn a little about their culture. We had some F-15Ds which was a two-seater version of the F-15C, and we gave orientation rides to some of their Ground Control Intercept (GCI) controllers.

I flew one of those flights on a standard profile, which was a full afterburner climb to 15,000 ft. of altitude. As I began my pull up into a 60-degree climb, I told my back seater to look back between the two tails (goal posts) for a good view of the field. Not used to that type of flying, his stomach didn't do well. When we shut down the engines after the flight, he was kissing the concrete, glad to be back on the ground. One day my Runway Supervisory Unit (RSU) Officer was late from lunch and missed the first afternoon takeoffs. Soon thereafter, the operations officer approached me, asking why he was late. I said he was eating. He repeated "Eatiiiing!!!" in a loud voice and stuck his finger in my chest. At that time, I was glad that I had received harassment training at The Citadel!

My first opportunity for an ocean crossing was to fly back from Eglin AFB after firing an air-to-air missile at a subscale drone (about 1/5th the size of an F-15). This provided for aircraft and missile testing, as well as pilot training. The missile I got to fire was the AIM-9L. The missile came off the rail, did a quarter turn, then flew an arc to the target, knocking off the pod on the wing tip. It was nice to know that your missiles worked, in case you had the need to fire them in combat.

My second opportunity for an ocean crossing was a factory pickup. I had to fly commercial to St. Louis to go to the McDonnell Douglas factory with three wingmen to pick up and lead back to Germany, four brand new F-15Cs. The routine was to rest or sleep during the day and report for the flight brief in the evening, meaning that after a 12-hour flight, we would land at Bitburg during daylight hours. The first attempt was aborted because one of the new aircraft had a hydraulic problem on start. Disappointed and wide awake at 9:00 p.m., we went back to the hotel, hung out in the jacuzzi, and tried to stay awake allowing us to sleep during the day and be fresh for the next attempt at night. The flight surgeon gave us no-go pills to help with that process. The next evening, we went through the same drill, but this time one of the four planes had a generator problem. These aircraft had been thoroughly ground and flight tested. Although they smelled like showroom cars, they all had six to eight flying hours on them. These two aborts also affected the three KC-135 tanker aircraft involved, one of which was already airborne.

Finally, on the third attempt, we got all the four F-15s to the end of the runway and off towards Germany. The first KC-135 met us over New York and gave us all a top off, filling all our tanks. Soon after going "feet-wet,"(flying over water), we joined up with our second tanker, who would "drag" us across the "pond." We had to refuel often enough to ensure that if for some reason, we could not get fuel, we could make it to a divert airfield. When I made a fuel check climbing through 23,000 ft. of altitude, my number three man's radio call sounded like his pressurization was not working. I asked him if everything was OK in his airplane, and he said yes. With no good reason to turn back, we pressed on without incident.

Until we left the last tanker over Scotland, our aircraft were restricted to the much slower tanker speed to refuel. By the time we had crossed the Atlantic Ocean, we had conducted six night refuelings, eaten two sandwiches, drank two soft drinks, and filled up three or four "piddle packs." After two false starts and a thirteen-hour duty day, I slept a full twelve hours from the time I put my head down, vowing I would prefer in the future, to get 12 hours of flying time on eight individual flights in lieu of from a single ocean crossing. The deployments to Decimomannu AB were where we got our best training. We had nice long setups, giving us a chance to work the radar. We also had a fully supersonic range, with ACMI pods and debrief to validate our shots, and the Aggressors for DACT instead of fighting each other in the subsonic TRAs. Our squadron deployed with another squadron on one of these deployments, and I was the project officer for the Tigers. To raise the bar, I set up a kill ratio contest with the other F-15 squadron, keeping score on a butcher block easel as to who had the highest kill ratio against the Aggressors. Our squadron came out on top with 5 to 1. It was not as good as the 10 to 1 ratio of the Korean war, but much better than the 1 to 1 ratio of the end of Vietnam. And to top it off, our two squadrons were fighting the best adversaries in the world.

Another Decimomannu deployment was interesting for a different reason. We arrived on a Saturday and were not flying until Monday. This gave us the chance to all pack into a 28-passenger bus Sunday and go to the beach for a day outing. The only problem was that our assigned driver from the motor pool decided to party along with the crews. During our return trip, he was going too fast around a curve and flipped the bus one and a half times ending up in the ditch. I remember the bus rotating around me while I hung on to a seat bar the best I could until I came crashing down. I was thinking at the time that I could not get hurt, because I wouldn't be able to fly. We all evacuated back to the clinic on the base and processed one at a time through the corpsman and flight surgeon for a real live mass casualty exercise that was not an exercise. When they asked me if I was OK, I said yes. As it turned out, all I had were a few sore (maybe slightly cracked) ribs that limited me to five "g"s during the dogfights. This was probably to my advantage, making me fly a bigger circle against the Aggressors and maintain my energy. The senior captain on the bus faired much worse as he took the wrap for not having the bus driver slow down.

Another major training event for me was the Tactical Leadership Program (TLP) conducted at Jever, Germany. This was a three-week program with one week of academics and two weeks of flying. The graduation day was a 16-ship low level flight with near simultaneous multi-axis attacks on a target, thwarted by air defense interceptors, such as our Bitburg F-15s and two F-4s from Munich who provided air defense. Was life good or what! The entire flying program worked up to graduation day. I had rented a cabin on the North Sea and brought my family up. The flying went well up until my wingman and I were doing a low altitude cross-turn to attack a four-ship of Dutch F-5s below our altitude. I was not the flight lead of record, but I had the tactical lead at the time. It was the fifth intercept of our flight at low altitude, and we had been working hard to give the enemy attackers a run for their money. On this last intercept, my wingman must have G-LOCed ("g" force induced loss of consciousness) and fatally flew into the ground without a radio call or any other indication he was having a problem. When I looked at my three o'clock position and saw he was not there, I called for him to check in on the radio. When he didn't respond, I turned back, and I saw the smoke from his crashed aircraft rising. I flew back to the site, circling and looking for his parachute or any other indication that he had made it out of his aircraft to no avail. I was occupied at the time acting as on-scene commander, but as I flew back to Jever AB when my fuel got down to fumes, I went into total shock from losing my wingman. By this time, a NATO AWACS (Airborne Warning and Control System) aircraft had arrived to take over the surveillance duties and confirmed the pilot hadn't ejected. Losing a pilot is tough on a squadron and on a personal level. Unfortunately, this training had a set timeline to complete, and the wing provided a replacement pilot and airplane, allowing me to finish the program.

Toward the end of my Bitburg career, I moved up to wing headquarters as Chief of Wing Scheduling. A captain from the 525th TFS Bulldogs and I planned all the Bitburg local flying a week in advance. On flying days, we would monitor flying, and if weather started deteriorating, made updates to TRA assignments in real time. Once, the wing was behind on flying time and needed to catch up, but you could not overfly the aircraft into a state of disrepair without sufficient parts. The way around this limitation was that you could preorder parts if you had planned a wing-wide training exercise. I planned our exercise and named it "Eagle Thrust." I had to brief it to the USAFE DO along with my wing commander. It turned out to be a huge success.

A fantastic and memorable event that the German government sponsored was a trip on the troop train to Berlin for the U.S. pilots and their wives. Much like the movies, Soviet soldiers were along the tracks, and they came on the train to check our passports. Once there, we got to see the sites, such as the Brandenburg Gate, Berlin Wall, and Checkpoint Charlie, where we crossed into East Berlin. What stuck out on the trip was the stark contrast between East and West Germany. As we crossed over into East Germany with our escort, we saw a lady selling blue and white porcelain boy and girl salt and pepper shakers on the side of the street. The price for one set was just a under $10.00 but represented a month's salary for an East German. I got a set, which I still have, and another to send back to my parents.

My 'fini,' or last flight at Bitburg, was a 1v1v1 in the TRA. What this exercise entailed was splitting up and flying to a corner and turning back into each other using radar and eyeballs to kill and not be killed. This demanded your best skills as a fighter pilot. By this time in my career, I had flown only fighters for nine continuous years, following my one short year in the T-33. I know *Call Sign: Kluso* alleges that your highest skill level is reached as a captain, and in general, that is true. In my case, I had only been a major for a short time but ended up winning the 1v1v1 fight by shooting down the other two F-15s and not getting shot.

I always joke with my kids. We all watched the first Top Gun movie together many Christmases. I always asked them, "Who's the best pilot?" It is no joke that today it is no longer me. It is, in fact, my son Matt. He's 44 years old and already has flown over 12,000 hours! He will be upgrading to captain soon for American Airlines, having come up through the ranks of flight instructor, turboprop and jet regionals to main line Boeing 737 and yes ..the Max 8.

When I had just pinned on my major's oak leaves, I investigated the possibility of joining the Israeli Air Force as my tour at Bitburg ended, which would have kept me in the F-15. There were two drawbacks. The first was that once you turned thirty years old, you could only instruct, meaning no more combat. The second was that you had to give up your U.S. citizenship and become an Israeli citizen. Neither condition sounded like the right answer. It is said that an Israeli fighter pilot is not getting effective training unless he is fighting at least three adversaries at the same time. I would have liked to have joined their ranks. This was another defining moment, but I decided the U.S. Air Force is where I wanted to stay.

With my three-year tour ending, I knew I would be getting a new assignment soon. The Air Force believed in "career broadening" and in general felt that at this point in a pilot's career, he needed to go to the staff. This also was a defining moment because I didn't want to leave the cockpit. I coordinated with the Soesterberg AB leadership, and they wanted me to come on board. They were a very experienced F-15 outfit and they wanted to keep it that way. My wing commander told me that career wise it would be better for me to bite the bullet and go to the staff, but that he would support me trying to stay in the cockpit.

Reluctantly, I made the career choice to go to staff, vowing to get back into the cockpit as soon as possible. There was an Army two-star who wanted the next fighter pilot with jump wings coming out of Europe to come to Fort. Benning to be the Air Liaison Officer (ALO) there. I had jump wings but didn't want a second dose of Fort. Benning. I had even jumped out of a C-141 that my father was flying. I bit my tongue on the equipment drop, ending my airborne training in pain on the last jump. Major General John McBroom, then Major McBroom, saved my bacon and diverted me to the Pentagon finally. It was good to have someone I knew from the past (Goose Bay AFB) working my assignment. I found out later that there had been a struggle between the division chiefs of International Aircraft Sales (PRIP) and Armament and Avionics Requirements (RDQA) for my presence. I later found out that my Bachelor of Science from USAFA was the silver bullet that got me RDQA.

Official U.S. Air Force photo taken at the Pentagon. (Air Staff Photographer, the Pentagon, Washington, D.C., Jan 1985)

Chapter 7

Supporting Blue Four at The Pentagon

If you must be in a staff job in the Air Force, doing it at the Pentagon is the best place to have an impact, in my opinion. It is a chance to shape the Air Force and support Blue Four. Blue Four is usually the least experienced wingman in a four-ship formation, who can use all the support he can get. Getting settled into the Washington D.C. area is a major challenge if you have a family and want to spend no more than an hour getting to and from work. Also, for the family, the schools were best in Fairfax County. For me that would mean Springfield, VA. I found that each additional ten minutes of commute subtracted another $10,000.00 of price of a house starting from a certain point. The trick was finding the right compromise between price and commute time.

At that time, in 1982, interest rates were 16.5 percent, but my real estate agent finally convinced me that the tax deduction would allow me to survive buying a three-story townhouse in Springfield. She also donated a Stihl chainsaw, so I could cut firewood to heat my house in the winter. The commute was at least an hour to the Pentagon going north on I-95 in the normal traffic lanes. The way to beat the "system" was by taking a bus. Buses were allowed in the center lane, cutting the 13-mile one hour commute down to 25-30 minutes. Another way to beat the system was to stand in the "slug line'" which was at the bus stops, where a carpool who had one member absent for TDY (temporary duty) or vacation would pick you up to make a fourth, getting to use the center fast lane. Slug lane commuters had certain rules, which were mostly to get in, keep quiet, and graciously accept a free ride in exchange for giving the driver the right to use the fast lane. Like *Groundhog Day - 1993*, there was no carryover or reservations.

For most Air Force assignments, in-processing and out-processing at the beginning and end of a tour were painful processes with all the fun in the middle. For the Pentagon, it was just the opposite. The initial in-processing and final out processing were quick and easy with the pain in the middle. What was interesting was the civil servant who in-processed me for my records check had, in fact, in-processed my father 25 years earlier. For a fighter pilot, the prospect of three to four years without flying was grueling. For those aspiring officers who were only career minded, they could "camp out" at the Pentagon, receiving two and even three promotions. Except for a few administrative positions held by sergeants, the entry level was major to serve as an "action officer." A division, with four letters, such as RDQA, normally consisted of a colonel division chief and ten action officers.

As an action officer, you built "packages" (your initiative with a staff summary sheet for coordination on top) and got sign-off from any other division who might be affected by the action. Then you got sign-off at the two star, then three star level. At the Pentagon, you quickly found out that "they" was "you." In the field, we always wondered who "they" was who were making all the rules, regulations, and policies. At the Pentagon, we quickly found out "they" was "us." Also, there were only about twelve fighter pilot action officers at the Pentagon at any one time, out of the 23,000 people who worked in the world's largest office building. The first thing they told me was I would have to learn how to talk without using my hands if I was going to get anything done at the Air Staff.

As I was in-briefed by a fellow fighter pilot, I was told that we would work with each other to get our initiatives through and wouldn't throw each other under the bus. Fighter pilot requirements mostly came from Langley AFB, home of TAC. Sometimes requirements could be pushed down from the Office of the Secretary of Defense (OSD) and sometimes you, as an action officer could get your initiative funded if TAC agreed. OSD requirements might not "stick" if they didn't have the required support at TAC.

Once you had a place to live, a way to get to and from work, and were in-processed, you had to learn how to navigate the building. Time was money when getting your package staffed. You could walk between any two points in the building in close to five minutes if you knew the short cuts. The building had five floors, five rings and a basement. The basement was not laid out the same as above ground, with many pathways blocked off for maintenance facilities or secure vaults. Arriving at the purple water fountain meant that you were in the vicinity of the Directorate of Operations (DOO), a location where many packages needed coordination. A shortcut across the center court could cut transit time in half, to keep you within five minutes. This skill was necessary because you could not move your action in a reasonable time by placing it in distribution.

The rule of thumb was that it took six months to become effective in working the building. Another rule of thumb was that budget protection was critical. The Air Staff could be cutthroat! If you went on vacation, even the action officer sitting in the next cubicle or office would steal your budget. As a Program Element Monitor (PEM), you were responsible for protecting your budget as it progressed through the board process, into the Program Objective Memorandum (POM), getting added to the two-year budget, and finally to congress for approval and appropriation.

Most of my actions were related to either executing approved requirements against the current budget or getting new requirements approved to be put in the budget. These packages would need to go through 12-15 offices to get approved. As I mentioned, using the distribution system wasn't timely, and you lost visibility to where your package was (which office in the process it was, and physically who had it on their desk). I found it more expeditious to literally walk my packages to each office, hand it to someone, and ask when they thought it would be approved. This helped with expectation management, and I knew exactly where my packages were always.

Early in my tour, I was assigned the action to clean up the Seek Eagle process, used for certifying new stores on all the aircraft intended to carry them, whether it was a fuel tank, a new weapon, or a rack to carry a weapon or sensor. Seek Eagle was managed by five separate, confusing, and sometimes conflicting regulations.

My task was to review the individual regulations, determine the requirements, resolve ambiguities, validate each aspect of them, clarify the intent and to create one consolidated regulation. Once completed, staffing the package was much easier than writing it because it didn't involve money. This was a huge undertaking that took two months, but my long hours paid off with this regulation being adopted as the new Air Force Standard. It's a little ironic, because my father had done the exact same thing 25 years earlier with five different flying regulations, standardizing them into a single regulation, Air Force 60-1. Streamlining the Seek Eagle process was my first of many accomplishments at the Pentagon.

When arriving for duty, my boss, Chief of RDQA , Colonel Bob Chandler, said he was going to make me his "Europe" guy. This meant that whenever there was a fighter pilot issue where our NATO or European allies were involved, I would be the action officer. This made sense since I had majored in Western European Studies at USAFA, lived and worked in England and Germany, lived in France, spoke French, and had a master's degree in International Relations. The family was supportive of the long hours and the tight budget from living in the Washington D.C. area. We enjoyed the many Officers Clubs and the Bolling AFB club had a great brunch.

My family at the Bolling AFB Officers Club Sunday Brunch. From left to right: Scott III, me, Patty, Jennifer, and Matt (Photographer unknown , Bolling AFB, Washington, D.C., circa 1985)

My first big action that involved budget and related to Europe was to support the OSD Family of Weapons Memorandum of Understanding (MOU). Under this MOU, the U.S. would develop the Advanced Medium Range Air to Air Missile (AMRAAM) and our European partners would develop the Advanced Short Range Air to Air Missile (ASRAAM). My role was to get the ASRAAM requirement approved. OSD would push the funding for integration on our fighters into the budget.

I attended meetings at the Pentagon, Whitehall, in the UK, and in Bonn, Germany to coordinate the requirement that had to be approved by the German government legislature, Royal Navy (RN) and Royal Air Force (RAF), U.S. Air Force, and U.S. Navy. At our working-level meetings, my missile engineer and I wrote the requirement to optimize the missile performance for launch at 450 knots of airspeed and employment at 15,000 ft. of altitude. These were the probable conditions of launching the weapon in a turning fight into the aft Weapons Engagement Zone (WEZ) of the target aircraft. aircraft. The challenge, after we agreed at our level to every word in the document, was to sell it to our acquisition leadership. In the case of Germany, it was all the way to the legislature. I was the overall lead for the project, but I also had to sell it to a board of two-star Air Force generals called the Requirements Review Group (RRG). Failure was not an option for any of us, because it would throw us into a delay for meeting the timeline for industry to develop the weapon.

To prepare for my presentation, I had to write out my brief on paper and have our Air Staff graphics department build the view graphs. Any changes in staffing the briefing involved going back to graphics and getting new viewgraphs. I had to anticipate potential questions and be prepared to go "two deep" on the answers; i.e., answer questions that might arise to my responses. All of us were successful in our endeavors in our separate services and countries and the requirement was signed by all the parties at the two-star and above level.

I discovered later that the ASRAAM requirement was not supported by TAC. They preferred to stay with the U.S. manufactured AIM-9 series of missiles (short range, dogfighting air-to-air heat seeking missiles), meaning the ASRAAM missile program was not adopted by U.S. forces. However, it is in service in the Royal Air Force (RAF), Royal Australian Air Force (RAAF), and some of their allies, replacing the AIM-9 Sidewinder.

My areas of responsibility at the Pentagon included the short range weapons of missiles, guns, gunsights, and even drones destined to be shot at by Air Force fighters. I protected keeping a gun on the Advanced Tactical Fighter (ATF) or F-22 aircraft. The Wright Patterson AFB community was in favor of a missile only fighter aircraft. The problem was that most head on fighter engagements may start with long range missiles, but if all targets are not killed, then a turning fight ensues, ending with a gun battle. We knew from the Israeli experience that 25 percent of their kills came from the gun. Even in Vietnam, we added the gun to the F-4D, making it into an F-4E. My goal was a better gun. The Air Force Gun Lab at Eglin AFB was developing a 23mm gun that was promising. I became their advocate at the Air Staff. All we needed was a buy-in at TAC to get a new gun for the ATF which evolved into the F-22.

My role was to brief the commander of TAC to get the support we needed to get the gun development incorporated into the ATF. The briefing took place at Langley AFB, at TAC headquarters. The result was that the commander of TAC approved the Phase 1, demonstration of the concept, but not the Phase 2 incorporation into the aircraft. I continued to advocate keeping a gun in the airplane which was at risk in some communities.

My next and biggest success turned out to be the new gunsight. At that time, all the century series fighters, such as the F-100, F-104 (short winged, high speed, single-engine jet interceptor), F-105, and F-4, relied on the Lead-Computing Optical Sight (LCOS). For the new all-aspect gunsight, the presentation on the windscreen was much more pilot-friendly and accurate. This concept had already been briefed at TAC requirements and was positively accepted. I felt that to be successful, it needed the support of the operators. The chief of the operations directorate (DOO) at TAC was Colonel Will Rudd, my previous boss at Homestead AFB. I contacted him and asked if he would be willing to go up to Binghamton, NY and fly the simulator with the new gunsight installed.

He agreed, and we headed to Binghamton shortly thereafter for the simulator demonstration. He flew the simulator and was able to get consistent gun kills on maneuvering targets within a couple of attempts. He was sold and helped get the TAC support to get it funded and keep it funded. The gunsight ended up in all the new fighter aircraft. Being a fighter pilot at my core, it was important for me to push this requirement to give pilots equipment to help them succeed in combat and their survivability. I feel that this is my biggest contribution in my career to Blue Four!

Another challenging, but rewarding project was to accept the tasking that came down to me from the Air Force Studies and Analysis Group (SAG). They need an Air Force fixed wing input to study a solution to counter one of the Soviet threat aircraft that could come across the Western Europe border. The results of our NATO sponsored Advisory Group for Aerospace Research and Development (AGARD) 14 study, led by helicopter engineers and one operator from the U.S., eventually pointed to the desired solution.

The challenging aspect was that the engineers could not get organized or stick to a timeline and agenda to get the study completed and briefed to NATO in the allotted time given. For us to be successful, I knew I would have to take the lead to keep us on track. Several of the engineers were excellent blackjack players and they had set up the schedule to meet in the major big cities in Europe that also had casinos as a fringe benefit. I was not part of the study until the third meeting, but I did profit, winning $225.00 playing off the hand of one of the better players at The Hague. We finished the study on time, and it was successful in supporting the solution. My director received a very positive letter of appreciation from the Studies and Analysis Group Director for my efforts, which was probably helpful in my getting promoted to lieutenant colonel early.

I was also the caretaker for the Air Force drone requirements. At that time the only mission in life for subscale and full scale drones was to serve as targets for weapons testing with the fringe benefit of pilot training. The Navy philosophy on subscale drones was to use them until they were shot out of the sky. The Air Force philosophy was to place infra-red pods on the wingtips which allowed the employment of infra-red (IR) missiles such as the AIM-9L or M, to knock off the pod and the drone could be recycled. Under my watch, TAC wanted to move from the heavier more expensive BQM-34-A Ryan Firebee II subscale drone to the slightly lighter weight, subscale MQM-107. A subscale drone is about 1/5 the size of a full-scale target, which is an aircraft that has been taken out of inventory and turned into a remote-controlled target. The latter met enough of the requirements to make the lower cost very attractive.

While I was in the RDQA armament and avionics division, I sat in as a substitute for the Director of Requirements Executive Officer a few times. When he left the "building," I was asked if I wanted the position, in which I served a full 12 months. This was another time when choices define your destiny. My obvious answer was yes! My reporting official jumped from being a colonel to a major general. That meant my Officer Efficiency Reports (OERs) would be endorsed by the Deputy of Research and Development, a lieutenant general. I also would be joining the brotherhood of executive officers, which included the Exec of the Chief of Staff. With additional position comes additional responsibility. I was responsible not only for supporting the Director of Operational Requirements (RDQ), but also the ten division chiefs who worked for him. These division chiefs were responsible for anything new that was produced for all the commands in the Air Force. This included cargo, fighter, and bomber aircraft, as well as weapons, avionics, and even Intercontinental Ballistic Missiles (ICBMs).

As soon as I accepted the position, I interviewed with each of the division chiefs to see what I could do to make them successful. The bottom line was to keep them informed of the needs of the boss to whom we all reported. This was the Reagan era, which translated to a funded program as fast as we could write and validate a requirement. President Reagan was rebuilding the decimated military from the previous administration. I routinely saw more than $500B of new programs being worked on any given day. The job was demanding, and my boss was even more demanding. My philosophy was to always stay ahead of him to prevent any natural disasters. To do this I regularly opened the first safe at 6:00 a.m. and stayed until he left with his homework bag which was often after 7:00 p.m. To keep up my stamina I swam 45 minutes per day at the Pentagon Officer Athletic Club (POAC) and grabbed a salad from one of the many snack bars on the way back to my desk.

Commuting was no longer a problem nor was parking. At 5:30 a.m. in the morning and 7:30 p.m. at night, the "slow" lanes move just as fast as the center fast lanes. In fact, I arrived early enough that the rats were just leaving the Pentagon for the dumpster at the South Entrance where I entered the building. I would call it in each time, and they would get an exterminator each time. No one can say that the Pentagon is in not populated with a few rats. I was issued a parking pass and with my hours I-95 was wide open. One thing to remember about I-95 in Northern Virginia is that the government shuts down and sends everyone home at the sign of the first snowflake, because when the actual snow hits it can take four to five hours to drive the 12-20 miles home for the commuters. For commute insurance I kept a sleeping bag, toilet kit, and change of underwear to spend the night, but was lucky enough to never need them.

Upon arriving at 6:00 a.m., I would read the "Early Bird," which was a compilation of the articles of the key newspapers that related to whatever our divisions were doing and all the night's message traffic to RDQ, our office. I highlighted all key information for my boss' arrival around 8:00 a.m. and made copies for any affected division chief. That guaranteed that when they got a phone call from the boss at 8:05 a.m. on an issue affecting their division they already had the answer. This was part of my philosophy of staying ahead of what my boss needed. The same philosophy relates to flying! The best way to ensure a successful flight is to plan the flight and stay ahead of the plan as you fly the flight. Our directorate ran smoothly, and we started many new Air Force programs.

The boss came from the Strategic Air Command (SAC). The division chiefs from TAC listened to the boss and supported him at every step even with the massive slide-building requirement. The SAC background division chiefs still had one foot stuck in SAC headquarters at Offutt AFB, NE and would often be "invited" for Saturday morning remedial slide-building training. We normally didn't come to work on the weekend. The Chief of Staff of the Air Force avoided doing his work at the office on the weekend and each level below in the chain of command normally followed suit.

The pace was demanding, and I yearned to get back to flying. One day when reading the message traffic, I saw that there was a competition for the Thunderbird Lead and Commander position. I put together my best "package," including a cover with small photos of all the fighters I had flown to date. It worked and I got a respite from the Pentagon to try out for the position flying the F-16. I went to Nellis AFB to meet the team and deploy to Luke AFB with them to spend time during an actual show. Each of the seven finalists got to socialize with the team and fly formation from the back seat of a two-seat F-16. I was not selected but the USAF Tactical Fighter Weapons Center Commander asked me if I wanted to come to Nellis AFB. He said that he had other squadrons I could command. This was a defining moment! I thanked him, but said, "No Sir" wanting to wait for an F-15 assignment that would give me a chance to shoot down Russian Migs, which I was sure was imminent! It hurts to be wrong!

As a semifinalist, I am in between the then current lead, Lieutenant Colonel Larry Stellmon, and Lieutenant Colonel Hoss Jones. (Base Photographer, Nellis AFB, NV, circa 1985)

I turned down two other gracious opportunities from my directors while serving as the RDQ Executive Officer. They were career defining moments that turning down held open the path to fly the F-15 and having a chance for combat but were career limiting in nature. The first offer happened when my director went to Spain as the 17th Air Force Commander and asked if I wanted to go with him. That could have led to an F-16 squadron commander position at Torrejon AB. My thinking was I would rather fly air-to-air combat in the F-15 than ground attack in the F-16.

My next turn down was to the last director I worked for, who later became the commander of TAC.

When he took the job, he pulled me out into the corridor and asked me if I wanted to stay or go. Exec is a burn out job and I had put in 12-13 hour days for a year and really missed flying. I elected to not stay and wait for an assignment back to flying. The officer I had been training to replace me as RDQ Exec ended up retiring as a lieutenant general. I got to be the Operations Officer of the 12th TFS Dirty Dozen flying the mission of Offensive Counterair (OCA). At the time, I was happy with my choices, and I am still happy today!

Chapter 8

F-15 Dirty Dozen Standard for OCA

Having spent three years out of the cockpit, I required a refresher training course in the F-15. This was scheduled at Tyndall AFB, in Panama City, FL. I was also assigned to take a six-ride air-to-ground refresher course at Tyndall, to follow the air-to-air refresher training. We flew to the Warning areas in the Gulf of Mexico for the air-to-air course and to the bombing and gunnery ranges near Eglin AFB for the air-to-ground work.

Since I last flew, the aircraft had been upgraded with Continuously Computed Impact Point (CCIP) software that placed a "death dot" on your windscreen that indicated where you wanted your bombs to hit. This was like the software in the F-16 and even the software availed to the 555th TFS, or Triple Nickel during the Vietnam War. This software provided highly accurate results and the pilot no longer had to dial a mill setting in his reticle. The two courses translated into a four month assignment there. We got lucky in that the tourist season was at the end and we got a good deal on a Mexico Beach rental right on the ocean. I could sit on the deck and watch the Gulf of Mexico while studying the F-15 Dash-1 and the F-15 Dash-1-34.

The hurricane season in the Gulf of Mexico in 1985 was very active. The instructors flew the F-15s to safety and the students drove their families to safety. Each time, we drove to Alabama. We evacuated four times for three hurricanes including twice for the same hurricane that did a 180-degree turn in the Gulf of Mexico and came back to shore. For the first evacuation, we took both cars, the television set, and almost everything we owned. By the last evacuation, we took little more than a checkbook and a toothbrush being numbed to the whole process. Dodging a bullet, our gulf-front villa escaped damage and we departed at the end of the hurricane season in December for Kadena AB, Japan.

Our arrival at Kadena was an eye opening experience. We arrived in a large government chartered aircraft flown by World Airways. We ended up being processed through a passenger terminal sized for a C-130 aircraft. Even though it was December, we felt hot and dehydrated. Eventually we made it through customs and located our luggage. What we experienced next was probably an example of the best sponsorship program in the Air Force. Our sponsors were Major Warren (Tex) and his wife, Sherie Gillespie. They had us to their house for refreshments then took us to a house they had arranged for us to rent in a car that they had arranged for us to buy. He then gave me flight suits with all the patches sewn on and my Dirty Dozen scarf. Wonderful hosts to this day, they set up the first Dirty Dozen reunion in 2012 at Round Rock, TX. The highlight of the reunion was a visit to the Pacific War Museum, in Fredericksburg, TX.

Before moving into our house off base, we stayed in the BOQ. We arrived on December 23rd, and there was no chance for getting a Christmas tree. Getting in the Christmas spirit, we used red and green streamers to shape a Christmas tree and tacked our Christmas cards on the "tree" for decoration.

The primary mission of the Dirty Dozen was OCA. This meant we conducted fighter sweep (flying ahead of the strike package) and fighter escort (flying with the strike package to protect them from enemy fighters) to support ground attack. In addition, we sat alert at Osan AFB, South Korea, serving in a Defensive Counterair (DCA) mission like that of Bitburg AB, Germany. The rotation to Osan was a great opportunity to stock up on blue jeans and tennis shoes for the kids. This did not last forever, because after South Korea hosted the 1988 Summer Olympics, all the prices went up.

We also prepared for our wartime mission of supporting South Korea, in case of an attack from North Korea. This meant practicing deployments to Korea to set up operations and receiving our ORI in South Korea. In addition, a small cadre of us practiced for ground attack to allow us to switch roles once air superiority was achieved. With this practice, we got ready to do our secondary mission.

Our air-to-air training consisted of fighting against each other in similar 2 versus 2 (2v2) ACM, participating in exercises, going on deployments, firing live missiles and guns at targets, and flying in Cope Thunder exercises.

12th TFS Dirty Dozen falls into position for a squadron photo. Squadron Commander 'Duke" Combs and Operations Officer "Rooster" Saunders are ready to lead the squadron into combat. (Photographer unknown, Kadena AB, JA, circa 1987)

Cope Thunder was a joint, international exercise in the Philippines almost the scale of Red Flag flown out of Clark AB. Participating naval forces flew out of Subic Bay NAS.

Captain "Odie" Neubeck proposed and got approved my call sign of "Rooster" believing that Lieutenant Colonel Saunders was close enough to Colonel Sanders to make it a match. That call sign stuck and has been with me since the mid-eighties.

The first time I briefed the Dirty Dozen pilots, I told them I expected my pilots to fly hard and safe. It was my job to help make that happen. We had a charter to fly hard, right up to the limits of the aircraft and ourselves but not beyond, and we would also fly by the rules. My intended goal was that we would be the best if we worked at it and that we wouldn't lose anybody in the process. The plan worked. I didn't have to visit any widows of lost fighter pilots, because we didn't lose any from the Dirty Dozen under my watch. This was the first squadron I flew in except the 13th TFS Panther Pack in Thailand that didn't lose anyone. I cannot overstate the good feeling it gave me when I left for my next assignment!

The 2v2 similar training was much the same as anywhere else, but we did have fully supersonic airspace. We participated in exercises with our Japanese allies and even deployed to their bases, such as Nyutabaru AB, Japan where we flew a Cope North and Misawa AB, Japan where we supported their F-16 ORI conducted by the Inspector General (IG) from the Pacific Air Forces (PACAF).

The deployment to Nyutabaru was very interesting. We flew our F-15Cs against the Japanese

F-15Js and flew against the U.S. Marine F-4S's from Marine Corps Air Station (MCAS) Iwakuni not far from Nyutabaru AB. I was flying in the back seat of a Japanese F-15J one day and a Marine F-4S approached the front of our aircraft head-on close enough that I could hear its engines. When I got back on the ground, there was only one frame of gun camera film showing the F-4S as he passed close by. My Nyutabaru Japanese F-15 front-seat pilot didn't even see him. I called the Marine squadron's duty desk, and they interrupted the debrief to ask if any pilot recalled a close pass with an F-15. The response was validating the "Big Sky" theory (the sky is so big that you can't hit anyone), allowing us to live another day!

Another close call occurred during a mass weather recovery into Clark AB during a Cope Thunder exercise. A published mass recovery procedure was necessary because ATC didn't have the capacity to handle that many singles. We had to fly a constant speed of 300 knots to a specific radial and distance from the Clark AB navigation aid and start a standard rate (usually 20 degrees) right bank turn. During this recovery, the F-16 in front of me turned late spoiling the geometry of the recovery and causing me to pass very close by him as I flew the standard recovery. Another near miss was chalked up to the Big Sky theory!

My third near miss occurred when I was flying in formation with the KC-135 tanker nearby Kadena

AB while attempting to complete our currency requirements for night refueling. I was on the right wing of the tanker in the "observation" position, when suddenly I saw two long afterburner plumes from a RF-4 (reconnaissance version of the F-4 that can go very fast) that passed very close to my right wingtip. What had happened was that the RF-4 pilot had approached the tanker with too much overtake. Instead of following the correct procedure of reducing power and passing well below the tanker, he lit his afterburners and pulled full aft stick climbing through the tanker formation. This was a very dangerous situation. When I got on the ground, I called the duty desk of the 95th Reconnaissance (Recce) Squadron and asked for the operations officer, who had been my first sergeant when I was squadron commander of the 20th Cadet Squadron at USAFA. I briefed him on the situation and told him I wouldn't file a near miss report if he counselled the pilot. He agreed and that was the last of it.

We had good maintenance, but I still had an engine quit on me when I was straight and level returning to Kadena AB one day. I simply pulled back the throttle on the failed engine, pushed up the throttle on the good engine and recovered making a single engine landing.

When not on deployment, we trained hard during the week and went to the squadron bar called the Tally Ho bar on Friday at 5:00 p.m. I had plaques made up in the Philippines that had four key sayings:

- ***Migs were born to die*** (The Cold War could go hot at any time.)
- ***Dirty Dozen Standard*** (We had the highest standard of performance for anything we did.)
- ***Top Notch*** (Our squadron was the best, hands down.)
- ***Sierra Hotel*** (This was code for the kind of fighter pilots and spirit we had.)

Plaques I donated to the Dirty Dozen outlining our mantra. (Original photo by Colonel Scott "Rooster" Saunders, USAF (Ret), Indialantic, FL, July 15, 2022)

The wives joined in on the fighter pilot spirit and comradery. One night there was a Roman toga party for the entire squadron. Most Friday nights consisted of hanging out in the Tally Ho with maybe dinner at the Officers Club called the Skoshi KOOM (short for the small Kadena Officers Open Mess).

On one occasion in particular, my wife Patty got really into the spirit of things and danced on the Tally Ho bar. My oldest son Scott III who is honoring the memory of the Tally Ho is reconstructing the bar in his Jackson Hole, WY house. It will be complete with many props including a mannequin dressed up in a flight suit with Dirty Dozen patches wearing a fighter pilot's helmet. Maybe a copy of this book will be laying on the bar!

My flying progression moved from a checkout as flight lead, to instructor pilot, to ultimately mission commander. Being a mission commander meant you were qualified to lead 16 F-15s into combat, as well as direct your own four-ship activity. Our mission commander checkouts always took place at Cope Thunder, where a simulated "war" was conducted.

As operations officer my job was to oversee the flying operation by leading the pilots from the front, monitoring the schedule, and maintaining situational awareness. I expected my pilots to fly hard and safe. It was my job to help make that happen.

As Dirty Dozen Operations Officer, I was part of a team that was ready to go anywhere in the Pacific. (Photographer unknown, Kadena AB, Japan, circa 1986)

One time we deployed to Kwang Ju, Republic of South Korea (ROK) where the local business community leaders wanted to host our pilots into their homes. What this meant was that our polite pilots didn't refuse their hospitality that included very potent libations. That night, I sat with my scheduler at the duty desk and assessed each pilot as he re-entered the building. If he came in looking like he didn't belong on the morning flying schedule we moved him to the afternoon schedule. I believe this contributed to all of us returning home to Kadena AB safely.

One of my favorite deployments was to Andersen AFB, Guam, refueling on a KC-10 and leading a six-ship formation. Our adversaries had already flown into Andersen. The deployment was to be kept quiet and I felt I didn't have to report any activities back to the DO at Kadena for security reasons. At the end of the deployment, he told me that I should have been giving daily reports. How does the saying go, "It's better to beg for forgiveness than ask for permission?" Guam was a paradise of sun and sand, and we had a good time during our non-working hours.

Just as we had the "Thief" at Udorn for making us fighter pilot clothing, we had a shop called "F-37" in Angeles City just outside the gate at Clark AB that made mementos out of wood. He hand-carved and painted plaques for us to hang on the wall in the squadron. He also made models of the airplanes we flew. His wares were renowned around the world.

These are the units in which I spent my fighter pilot operations career and support years. Also pictured is my squadron commander sword from USAFA. (Original photo by Scott "Rooster" Saunders, Indialantic, FL, circa 2021)

With my time at Kadena coming to an end, I knew I would probably be leaving the cockpit for the second time. I had taken Air War College (AWC) by correspondence, as I had done for Squadron Officer School (SOS) and Air Command and Staff College (ACSC). My theory had been to do the professional military education (PME) courses by correspondence minimizing my time out of the cockpit. Conventional wisdom was that attendance in person for the senior service school was a good thing. I was sitting alert at Osan AB, ROK, when I got the dreaded phone call that meant I was leaving the F-15 and the Dirty Dozen. I was on the senior service school list and had been selected for Paris, France, at École Militaire.

I would be completing two courses. The first one was the *École Supérieure de Guerre Aérienne* (Superior School of Air Warfare), slated for 12 months and the second one was the *Cours Supérieur Interarmées* (Superiour Interarmy School, or Senior Joint Warfare School) lasting four additional months. The courses were all in French, with the plan that I would go to the Defense Language Institute for thirty days enroute. I had taken French in school, from the third grade up to my first class year at USAFA and tested for language proficiency as a lieutenant at Homestead AFB. I had even served as the project officer for our squadron exchange with the French Air Force Fighter Squadron 2/5 Ile-de-France, from Orange-Caritat AB, France, but I was rusty. I explained to the personnel officer that the French believe in their language like we believe in our Flag. I argued that to be effective as a U.S. Air Force ambassador, I need more French training.

The next thing I knew, I was assigned to take both the basic French language course and the intermediate French language course, together lasting twelve months. This was a defining moment by opening my big mouth! I would now be out of the cockpit for two and a half years at a minimum. I violated Rule 3) *Eighty-twenty.* I lost a potential year of flying by not keeping quiet. Every dark cloud has a silver lining. I did win the Commandant's award for being the top student that year for the entire Romance Language department and I did have fun in Paris, experiencing the French sphere of influence in the world and making some life-long friendships.

Epilogue

Following my F-15 Eagle tour in the 12th TFS Dirty Dozen Fighter Squadron, the Air Force selected me to attend the Defense Language Institute in Monterey, CA to master the French Language followed by attendance at École Militaire (the French War College). These were career broadening opportunities but ended up meaning the end of operational flying.

I did receive the honor of a backseat Mirage 2000 flight piloted by Colonel (retired as General) Charles Ricour at Dijon AB, France while at the French War College. This may have been a reward for my thesis on the Creation of a French Aggressor Squadron, which was awarded the highest score ever received by a foreign student. The French Air Force didn't adopt it because the Berlin Wall came down and the Cold War ended in 1991, while I was in school. In addition, I also maintain a close relationship with my former roommate on War College trips and confident, Colonel Patrick Gaviard (retired as General). Before he retired, he received the *Commandeur de la Legion d'honneur* from President Chirac, standing for *Honneur et Patrie* (Honor and Country).

He accuses me of not wanting to come back to Paris just because two Romanian girls stole my wallet which I had moved to my front pocket for security reasons. It did not save me, as they still got all my euros for the day that I had stashed away. One of the girls took them out and threw the wallet on the floor of the Metro while the other one tried unsuccessfully to push my wife to the ground to distract me.

General Patrick Gaviard receives the prestigious Commandeur de la Legion d'honneur award from President Chaques Jirac. (Photographer unknown, Paris, FR, November 1999)

Happily, I was returned to flying after school as the 325th Operations Group ADO at Tyndall AFB getting a full F-15 RTU Instructor Course checkout. It was not operational flying, but it was still the F-15, and I had the chance to participate in some realistic training exercises. I had the good fortune to lead a detachment of F-15s from Tyndall AFB to fly against the Top Gun F-14 Tomcats at the Navy's Fighter Weapons School in

Miramar NAS, San Diego, CA. The F-15s won, of course!

In addition, I was selected as Blue Force Commander and Joint Forces Air Component Commander (JFACC), leading our forces to victory in Operation Roving Sands 92 at Biggs AFB in El Paso, TX. During a local television interview, I told the reporter, "The Blue Forces will win." I did lead air forces, army forces and Army National Guard forces to a victory over the Red Forces!

I was also assigned to Seoul, Korea as Executive Officer for the U.S. Forces Korea (USFK) Deputy Commander in Chief (DCINC)/7th Air Force Commander for exercises. There I served as the JFACC and Night Air Operations Commander during exercises in the Seoul Command Post. While there we deployed to the on-site command post for incursions of the South Korean border seven times.

An incredibly significant moment for my future in aviation happened when I was attending an Air Show at the Melbourne, FL airport. My wife Patty had passed away, and I was there with my current wife Rhonda. When I saw a Waco biplane flying, something stirred in my soul. I looked at Rhonda and told her I was getting back in the air! I proceeded to refresh my CFI and obtain my Certified Flight Instructor-Instrument (CFII) and Multi-Engine Instructor (MEI) ratings. Since then, I have added over

1,400 hours to my 3,800 Air Force hours in various single-engine and multi-engine aircraft, given instruction, and flown many hours in my Mooney M20J named "Tootsie."

"Tootsie" has taken us all over the U.S. and the Bahamas, as well as being my primary Angel Fight transporter and platform for flight instruction. (Original photo by Scott "Rooster" Saunders, Rome, GA, circa 2017)

My wife was the one that suggested I buy my Mooney. My good buddy, Lieutenant Colonel Rick "Kluso" Tollini (who wrote the book Call-Sign Kluso) calls the Mooney the Porsche of general aviation. I agree wholeheartedly! Rhonda also named my new flight instruction business as "Scott the Fly Guy," which has been active for eight years, and now includes Gerardo Mesa, who I fly with frequently for training and Angel Flights. I've been blessed to fly more than 125 Angel Flights for Angel Flight West, Pilots for Christ, Servant Air Ministries, and Mercy

Flight Southeast taking patients to and from doctor's appointments when they had no other means. The amount of gratitude these patients express is unparalleled.

As in military aviation general aviation can present aircraft issues. I had several such issues. The first bunch occurred in a Sierra purchased by a charity organization for which I flew. The first one involved an electrical fire on take-off with smoke coming out of the instrument panel, and Rhonda saw the smoke first. As I was in the initial climb-out, I simply pulled the power back and did a 180-degree turn and returned to the field safely.

The second major Sierra issue was when I was returning from a hurricane relief mission in Texas when I encountered a propeller overspeed at night causing me to lose power at 6,500 ft. of altitude along with the heading indicator and radios. I was able to glide into Fair Hope, AL successfully with a power-off landing. I even had no brakes, topping off the emergency. Thank goodness for long runways and for on-speed landings. Finally, I was flying my Mooney from San Jose, CA to Denver, CO because when I was working a proposal for Lockheed Martin. Flying at 17,000 ft. of altitude over the Rocky Mountains, I suddenly lost power and began to descend. I began to circle while attempting to regain power. Soon a green plateau emerged below for my emergency landing. (I was thinking at the time before I saw a place to land that I had had a "good run!") At 14,000 ft. of altitude though, my power came back. Working with Denver Center ATC, I got vectors into Montrose, CO where a top engine mechanic revealed to me that I had one loose bolt on my magneto box. It is amazing what a loose bolt can do in an aircraft. The aircraft also needed an exhaust manifold. A week later, I returned from Denver to Montrose and recovered my Mooney.

The FAA recently bestowed their highest honor upon me with the Wright Brothers Master Pilot Award for 50 years of safe flying without pilot deviations! This was a real honor because most of us GA pilots are always wary of getting our hands slapped by the FAA.

Bob Jex, of the Orlando Flight Service District Office (FSDO) FAA presents me with the Wright Brothers Master Pilot Award for 50 years of safe flying with no deviations, with my wife Rhonda by my side. (Photo by Sean Holloway, Bartow Airport, FL, August 2019)

I continue to instruct flying to PPL and CFI students, as well as conduct biannual flight reviews, instrument proficiency checks, and complex aircraft checkouts. I also fly patients to their doctors when they have no other means to get to their appointments. Finally, I enjoy flying to vacation spots and to see family, and fly to reunions, such as the 18th TFW in Colorado Springs and the 36th TFW in San Antonio, TX.

The bottom line is that I will always be a fighter pilot and continue flying as long as I can. I have enjoyed serving my country, my students, and my patients who need air transportation.

Kent Haley assists me in flying a patient and his wife, Ray, and Sharon Hershey to their doctor in my 1980 Mooney M20J. The flight was on July 28, 2019, from Fort Meyers, FL to Jacksonville, FL. (Photographer unknown, Craig Airport, FL, July 28, 2019)

God has spared me through many aircraft emergencies and near misses. I believe he is not finished with me, and there's more yet to do. I hope you have enjoyed my story.

A Diary Through Spirit

Lesley G Shepherd

Clairvoyant Author and Tutor for Spirit

An autobiography of channelled scripts
given from the spirit world with
Dear Reader extracts
from the author's
Guiding Lights

May the light shine in your heart forever

LH

First published 2011
Reprinted 2015

© L. G. Shepherd

A CIP catalogue record for this book is available
from the British Library.

ISBN 978 0 9568182 0 1

All rights reserved. No part of this publication may be reproduced, transmitted, or stored in a retrieval system, in any form or by any means, without permission in writing from the publisher, nor be otherwise circulated in any form of binding or cover other than that in which it is published and without a similar condition being imposed on the subsequent purchaser.

All those depicted in this book from both planes of life have given their permissions and blessings to the author for their words to be included in this book.

Lesley G. Shepherd has asserted her right to be identified as the author of this work in accordance with the Copyright, Designs and Patents Act 1988.

Front cover – these are my personal guides, beautifully illustrated by Lyn Cottrell. To the left my first gatekeeper and to the right my healing guide from Atlantis origin. Notice the colour of her eyes.

Contents

Illustrations

Preface

My humble beginnings as a scriptwriter for spirit started with communications through the pen to paper while innocently pausing to write to a friend in Devon when quite unbeknown to me, with scribbles, my first ever communication began. At this time I had no connection with anyone who could guide me in this new phenomena and I had never read any books of a spiritual nature either.

The only recollection with being inquisitive to the paranormal was making an Ouija board with loose numbers and letters on scraps of paper. I was about 20 years old taking a holiday with my then fiancé, now husband of 42 years, my parents and younger sister Barbara, my Auntie Madge, Uncle George and their daughter Julie, who is sadly now in spirit passing in her early forties. We were staying in a chalet at Highcliff near the New Forest and Bournemouth. The men had gone down to the local pub and the women stayed in with the then young Barbara and Julie. We decided to amuse ourselves as in those days television sets were not found in holiday homes, also in those days, I didn't know the implications of "Ouija", and where unknown spirit entities come through to those on the earth plane; so with the upturned glass we placed our forefingers on the glass and after awhile circling around, a spelt out name came forward of a previous owner and we, in a highly amused state asked "where the bread knife was" that had been misplaced some days before. We were told to look behind the cooker to find it, and yes we did find it there the next morning. We were extremely lucky in contacting such a friendly spirit. I can remember being quite engrossed and fascinated along with my colleagues in crime (spiritually speaking) with more messages coming from other spirit entities. When the men came home in a high state of merriment knowing what we were doing they were looking through the windows tapping and giggling and, in high pitched voices saying "IS THERE ANYONE THERE?" After a short silence, words began to spell out that spirit was not amused at this and were quite angry for not taking them seriously, to which the glass flew off the table and smashed. I remember a sombre mood descended on those present.

My second warning of this nature happened while working for the G.E.C. telecommunications engineering division at Stoke, Coventry. During our lunch break, myself and two other secretaries, one of whom was having a troubled love life, hearing of my holiday exploits asked if we should have another go. I agreed only because she wanted her grandmother to come forward. As before, we set out the Ouija board and were just beginning when an engineer came storming into the office and asked us in a very concerned way, did we know what we were doing! Were we also aware of the implications of having a bad connection with spirit as there were low entities which could do us harm, as well as higher ones that are there to help and he told us never to open ourselves up to these elements until we protected ourselves. This was sound advice with hindsight.

The **Dear Reader** dialogue of advice comes from experience working with spirit and will be in ordinary print throughout. Direct dialogue communication from spirit friends and family will be in *italics* and dialogue from my Spirit Guides will be in script form with their corresponding sign offs.

CHAPTER 1

THE BEGINNINGS

As I refer to my letter writing episode and my first communication in 1988 with a different media, I was inquisitive but apprehensive. Firstly I was intrigued to know who and what the contact was to be. Over the next few days and weeks I persevered holding the pen in a firm but relaxed way and gradually the odd word came out and then stilted sentences after I had written – my name is Lesley what is yours.

I was fortunate in the contact being my long gone to spirit grandmother Gertrude Goodacre, my mother's mother who, as it turned out, had been chosen from spirit to look out for me and to protect me in my early endeavours with a closeness with my spiritual connections and family in the afterlife.

My gatekeeper guide must have been protecting my endeavours even then as I go back to those early encounters. As I recall another message of only writing what my intuitive thought was, and not putting in any extra words, or even stopping to correct the spelling, the flow improved, but as I read back my notes I found that as I asked a question only the answer was appearing and with the lapse of time the sense of the message was forgotten. I decided that I would connect only with my loved ones when imperative to do so. This was to become my mind-waves linking with spirits vibration.

From **script of 18.2.88** I found another contact coming in from my father's mother, telling me that due to his illness to ring him and that he needed help. My father had at this time lost the fight to keep his leg after an on going arterial problem. He was both strong mentally and physically when his health started to fail him, he got on with his life as always without complaining. I recall him actually pushing the vacuum cleaner around in his wheelchair and hopping out to the ambulance when they called for him to take him to hospital for physiotherapy. Being a stubborn man he didn't like his false leg and wouldn't wear it, it being one of the older heavier types that they fitted at that time. I am telling you this as a lot of his traits have rubbed off on me as the years ahead have proved.

Going back to the 18.2.88, as usual the messages were scrambled and mixed up although I felt that I was still in the presence of my family and the connections were solid. Whilst holding the pen script came through as follows, *"Help my Norman with his garden/ I think of him all the time, you are mummy's boy tell him."* They had asked me to be patient as my thought patterns and theirs were misaligned. I was told to vet what I was writing and only write that given by thought word for word so that I didn't repeat what they were giving me. I felt very excited that for once my scripts were beginning to make sense. I had asked if my father was to join her (my grandmother) on the astral plane but by pen she said not yet, make sure to persevere with this method of communication as it will help him when he does pass. She was worried about her wedding ring and this message, along with *to ring my father* I missed the point but she persevered with me until by March of that year we had quite good conversations. Script of 19.2.88 shows the evidence given (*mummy's boy*) was correct with him being her youngest child and my mother had always said that it had caused some marital friction in their very long marriage.

9.3.88 Script *(when your father goes on/I will be there/the moment of death/is not getting here/or the moment of torment/you are knowledgeable so I will tell you/I can see every relative that comes here/Norman will see me/he has some time yet/to get to know/what he will/might do to see me/world of beauty/and peace/so be careful not to disturb/I am pleased to know you) (my granddaughter is Lesley/go to Norman/and tell him/to look for my ring/thank you/bye for now).*

I had my two most precious links with the family. Within March of this year news in the spirit world must have got around my family links as week after week new connections started to flow in. I recall on 9.3.88 script from my father's brother who had passed before I was born in the 1940's, came through with *night time is my day* and his mother had given him permission to converse with me and with that he told me not to worry about my impending move and that it would happen quite quickly. Thus showing, that even when family go to the spirit realms they still, very much, want to be involved with family life here. In fact I now know this helps **their** bereavement process and they are able to move onto a higher vibration of life sooner. This message also had a signed off signature of Derek and a different handwriting to my other contacts.

Another startling message of the same date was from an old friend and neighbour saying (*go to my mother/she is not well/ mother is mourning.* Yes! *This is EDDIE/my message is/KISS/my little girl for me/will you please/*Yes! *Thank you*). This was a shock as I didn't know that he had died. My only contact was his ex wife Dot and after ringing her just for a chat she told me that Eddie had taken his life that morning and that she couldn't understand why. I asked her to come and visit me and I showed her the above script. After some consideration she asked me to try and contact him again. It worked. We found out that his second marriage had money problems and he had taken this way out, but having got to the spiritual dimension he had realised the heartache was still with him alongside his loved ones, including his beloved daughter who he was missing terribly. I had not known about this child as she was born to the second marriage. I did know of his only son (by his first marriage to Dot) as he was a friend of my sons' and had become a fine young man. Dot persuaded me to visit his mother who she was still very much in touch with. I did this and Eddie's mother invited me to the funeral so that I could pass on Eddies wishes. I remember picking his little girl up and kissing her and whispering, daddy sends you this. It was all very emotional for me and I didn't stay too long but that day I made a very firm promise to spend the rest of my life to help spiritual friends in any way I can till my years are done on this earthly dimension of ours. Very brave a promise as I now know they do hold you to such promises, but they also give you back so much joy too, especially if you like helping others to be happier with their lot.

Before leaving this episode in my life can I say that Eddie has in the preceding years been re-united with his ex wife through cancer and his only son of that marriage, through ironically a car accident. Incidentally Eddie had been taken tragically by ending his life by attaching a hosepipe to the exhaust. At that time, I felt as a friend, that if only he had been able to talk to someone he may not have died, hence my firm commitment to spirit that hopefully I will fulfil their high standards, as I am doing now, to connect with my fellow beings here on the earth plane. I have met a few people thinking like Eddie, lonely with the pill bottles lined up. A friend has given them my card and with the heavenly connection of their family they have made them see sense, I being only the instrument by which they can re-connect to them.

My personal connections with my family ties also help me to sort out emotions and stressful times such as moving in my case. They can often see ahead, that is, if you are wise enough to put your faith in them, which will let them help smooth life's passageway ahead.

I recall on my **24.3.88 script** (*yes! gran here/what do you want/ we think you will not/there is not a sale of the property you are to buy/but you will go to see another property very soon. You are very tired; you are not going to see things in the right light*). Signing off with, (*we are going / you are welcome / love you. x*)

Most unfortunately there is a gap of missing scripts from 1988 to 1993, either due to me not realising the importance of my scripts and thinking that the phenomena was only helping me with my life, instead of being a new way of life, which was to be proven in the years to come. Also no other family members had ascended in this time giving me a lull in my connections. The messages I received mostly in 1988 were personal ones giving me strength and guidance during a house move taking 5 to 6 years to complete as there were different breaks in the chain. At this time I was asking my family links to help keep me calm through this very stressful time. Also, my spirit family and friends were signing off each time and I diligently dated every piece and filed them away in a spring folder. This proved to my spirit family I was indeed listening.

They knew they could still link with their earthly family through this interaction with their thought and mind energy with the wonderful vibration that connects this plane of life with theirs. Time indeed to align my thought-wave patterns to make their links stronger and of course as 1993 approached my first recollections of close family going to the spirit kingdom was one shock after another and so awakening my awareness rapidly, to such an extent it become second nature to put pen to paper to witness their passing giving comfort both ways through the heavenly veil.

1993

Script of 6.7.93 My first unstilted message shortly after Dad (Norman) and my husband John's Auntie Helena's passing. They passed the same day within hours of each other and shortly after my mother-in-law said (*it's good here but tiring, I must rest now! Love to you and the family Mum H. xxxx x to Todd!* (The family dog) *Sarra!* (My daughter) *Glen,* (My son), *and the rest of the family, Xxxx, love you Toooooo…………..*) Then, after a short pause, very clearly (*I am here, please acknowledge*) I did so by thought (*one day when you're not too busy – yes it's me Dad Mullan – go to my mums' and plant the Gladioli's. Put them in for me*) I acknowledged then by thought that I would (*good! Many thanks Love you! Dad.*)

My recollection of my father's passing was of him being taken into hospital after a stroke. Within a few days he seemed to be making quite a good recovery, his strength as always coming from somewhere, even asking my husband John to help him shave so that he would look respectable. He asked to be moved out of his single room so that he could have company in the main ward, but the day after this move there was a sudden development where he had taken a tumble out of bed and had another severe stroke putting him into a comatose state. I persuaded my sister Barbara and her husband Brian to stay at home with a promise that I would call from the hospital if there was any further change.

As I sat by his side holding his hand I said to him with my mind (Dad, don't be afraid to move on, I will look after the family. You have suffered enough. It's time to go. I love you!). At this point the nurse on duty came along saying she wished to bathe and turn my father asking us to wait in the day room for a short while. I remember thinking to myself that this would make him uncomfortable as this was on his afflicted side. As we sat there listening to the hospital radio there was a news flash that an elderly lady, a Mrs Helena Coppage from Henley-in-Arden, had been hit by a lorry and killed immediately. Auntie Helena was always dashing around helping her neighbours and friends with their shopping so it was so like her to go in this tragic way. The name and place being unusual and my instincts by then quite acute, I turned to my husband and told him he should go and break the news to his mother as this was her only living relative. Then, as I walked up to the ward to revisit my father, the nurse came walking down towards me saying that unfortunately he had passed away peacefully whilst she was tending him. I asked if I could see him and she said it would not be pleasant as they had not laid him out properly and wouldn't I prefer to wait! I am so pleased now that I did not because I had my first sight of the spiritual cord being broken and I knew in my heart of hearts he would be strong enough to contact me as soon as he was able, and that was quite soon as it happened.

Many mediums have brought the message I gave Dad telepathically almost word for word through individual mediums at our local spiritualist church. I might add that I was encouraged to join the church to help me come to terms with my three dear losses.

At this time I was also made aware of a different hand writing where a non member of my family came in from time to time such as, *"Hello my name is Edna will you pass on a message to my daughter"* the message reads *"don't grieve for me/I am OK/you will contact me again/won't you/you will know me/going now love/ Bye Bye. Edna."* I'm ashamed to say that many messages were not passed on quickly enough as it took me some time to realise the significance of them. I could have given solace to the recipients much sooner. Also, was it a coincidence that I took over the post of church secretary from someone called Edna?

As I come to the 1993 part of my diary through spirit I started to get little snippets of spiritual life and as you progress Dear Reader through this book I will hopefully be able to give you a little insight into the realms we as mortals pass onto.

Script of 19.7.93 I had asked if Dad was there and I got, *"No. But you can speak to me, it's Grandad! What's wrong? You had a visitor last night that frightened you"* (I had indeed seen a shadow by my bed. I was startled and I rationalised that my father had tried to waken me) "Yes!" *Oh it's OK, we were aware, it was one of us that has not quite got the knack yet, do you understand? Sorry if he frightened you, it was not intended, he will try again but do try not to be afraid, is this OK? We were not able to protect you, sorry! It won't happen again, rest assured. We love you and you are not to worry. Going now love, God Bless you, you must rest now, speak to you again soon."*

My Dear Reader, from this text I deduced that it was not my imagination or inner thoughts speaking as now I know that indeed spirit has to conform to a certain code of conduct with mutual respect, as do we, in not using a spiritual connection for frivolous means.

Script of 7.7.93 I had taken my mother to church hoping for a connection with my father through a visiting medium and as we were sorely disappointed I put pen to paper and the reply was as follows – *"Yes. I know I'm a naughty boy! Next time! Perhaps. I still love you. What time did it start? 7.30 OK! Next time* (I might add that I now know there is no perception of time as we know it in the spirit realms and I only need to tune in just before the service for a connection, that is if I am lucky enough to be chosen by the medium.) Dad's script went on

"We had a big shindig here! One of us has gone up a level; I am on the Ground Floor. Only joking! Incidentally, one of us is good at healing, do you need this? All right, is tonight OK? One of us will see to it. (Even at this early stage in my development this reference to a healer I know as being a higher source of entity and vibration from the spiritual planes to which they can link with you on the matters of health for yourself or for a loved one, this vibration can be induced to help heal the living body). *Mum is not well I hear, is it bad? One of us will go and see!* (Mum was withdrawing from life a little and I told him this). *I know that! I have been around her. She has not got me there to make her? I am going to see her when I get better at this. Do you wish to go any further?* (meaning my spiritual pathway) *Good! We can help you! We are being told you are to communicate personally soon. We are on our own at the moment but our leader can help you to see with your sixth sense, one of our communicator's knows a lot of these problems! You are in good hands. PROTECTED. One of us is listening out for you at all times. You are on your guard too much, just let it happen. Your Mum H is coming through, she wants to tell her grand – daughter* (me) *not to worry as she is also protected by her family and good groundwork has already been done. She is not to worry, her house has been blessed.*

Goodnight and God Bless Lesley.
Signed Grand-Mum Goodacre.
Our guide! And Dad. Xxxxx. Goodnight."

Dear Reader. I was so pleased to be informed that my home was protected as well as myself during this testing time with spirit as I had heard of lower entities causing havoc with people's lives that had unwittingly drawn in such forces. Also, even up to the present day I am cautious to always make sure I draw my spirit family forward in my minds eye (Sixth Sense), whom I might add, gets bigger every day, for protection when picking up the pen as a spiritual form of communication known as automatic writing.

With reference to my mother in-law's passing, I recall the events as though it was yesterday. We had a phone call from my husband's father to say that thinking his wife was having a lie in he had gone to make her a cup of tea, then when taking this into her he tried unsuccessfully to awaken her. He had rushed to a neighbour's house who had at one time been involved with some kind of nursing and first aid. The neighbour realised after assessing the situation that she had had some kind of stroke in her sleep and they of course had sent for an ambulance. On her admittance we were told that she had suffered an embolism at the base of the brain and if she recovered she may sustain some physical disabilities which would seriously debilitate her.

I am telling you this Dear Reader, as I believe that everyone is allowed to depart from this world as he or she wishes on his or her final day of passing. Mum H (she allowed me to call her this, although strictly speaking she was my mother-in-law) had a very different passing to my father. She attended church socially on a regular basis and was used to friends passing on. I'm sure because she was a strong woman who had kept herself quite fit attending old time dances with and without Jess her husband, she chose her final day to go to plan.

My father in-law wished to stay overnight in case the worst was to happen. I volunteered to stay with him for company knowing that I could be of some comfort to him. With my beliefs becoming stronger day by day, week by week, month after month, even at this time not really knowing what was happening to me, I was getting stronger in my convictions that there must be more to life than this!

Anyway, there we were sitting in two chairs looking over mum, listening to the swish of the cooling fan. An occasional gurgle from mum seemed to punctuate our conversation to each other showing that even though she was on a spiritual level with her Etheric body, rather than her physical body, she wanted to be part of the conversation and to listen and watch us. I felt very close to her at this time. We were chatting about dad's grandchildren and how they were growing up, also how much mum was pleased with her other son Colin's match in a partner the second time around, bringing two more grown up children into our family fold. She was just starting to get to know them quite well as she and Jess were slowly letting go of their responsibility to Colin and his two children by his first marriage and how she approved of their union so much. At this point there was quite a loud gurgle. I do not feel on looking back that it was our imagination. Even dad remarked how she still wanted to dominate the conversation and boy did we laugh.

The next day mum was moved to another ward and the fan was removed and not given to her again. My husband and his brother thought that it was so cruel to move her and that the hospital staff were not paying her enough attention, but really they knew she would not last much longer. She waited till all the family had gathered around her, opened her eyes to look at us all in turn, closed them and passed peacefully away.

She often draws close to me when picking up the pen for a chat and I feel very privileged to be able to keep that close link for the family, keeping her abreast of all the happenings, good and bad, that go on from time to time, so that she is still very much a part of the family that she has had to leave behind. I know she would like her sons to connect with her one day, but as yet they are both shy of even contemplating this. I wait for this day. "What joy" for all three of them. I believe that everyone who wishes to communicate in this way, it has to be a two-way communication; unfortunately we on the earth plane seem to be in need of knowing it is taking place and want untold proof of its existence even when the bond is very strong.

Script of 19.7.93 started with some personal guidance with *"time has come to progress to better things for you, but don't be impatient though, it takes time. What way do you wish to go; my leader is asking me to ask you while you are communicating in this way. Insight will come to you too, to enable you to go to great lengths, following a true path laid out for you from spirit and only beckoning those who will not use you."*

Dear Reader, I conclude from this paragraph along with continuous script changes that were happening in my level of correspondence that help is always at hand through spirit and not always through a book of learning. This helps you with your understanding of life, of where you are coming from and where you want to be in the future. I have found that through the power of thought waves to spirit they indeed move mountains to achieve the goals you set out for yourself, as you will find out how my life progresses as you read on.

Another snippet on this day of communication *"Grandma says there are many things on this plane that are so different than that on the earth plane. We can perform miracles and we often do."* Also *"one of the Goodacres* (my mother Gwen's side of the family) *is coming through to let us know that our London friend is to be an ordinary human being* (This I took as a re-incarnation and then an astounding message came through) *"your friend next door is after leading him to the light,* (this from an Irish family member in spirit would have been said in this way) *ordinarily we wouldn't give you this information but Anne must be prepared so please take her to church with you as it is most important, we will guide you so that she will receive a message from him."*

Unfortunately Anne was not a believer of this form of communication and my hands were tied. I was able to comfort her and told her he sent his love. It is such a pity when this happens as when the spirit has been released to the higher existence the first thing that a risen soul wants to do is reach out and have it proven to them that they too can still communicate. This helps them with their desire to know that the family are all right and maybe comfort those left behind.

I recall David's passing. He was very ill for some time with cancer. I remember him having a good sense of humour when losing some of his very thick wavy hair and flirting with me asking would I still like him when he had none. I recall the evening when he died. I happened to be at church when his passing took place and when I returned home I found my husband in quite a state as he had tried to resuscitate him. He had rung for an ambulance several times but the delay was a half an hour or more. I told him he had done all he could it was just David's time to go. I believe again it was spirit's way to let David go with dignity at home as he would have wished. Also recalling that only the day before Ann had said he was lying in the conservatory with the dog listening to Mario Lanza, his favourite artist, who was singing "I Walk with God". The sunshine was streaming through and he looked so peaceful. I'm sure that every obstacle was put in the way that night to insure his passing happened in his own special way. I might add that my husband had been taught by the Saint John's Ambulance Brigade in his younger days the procedure for resuscitation so I know he would have done his best. Also it doesn't normally take an emergency 999 call so long to respond, the crew said they had been held up getting to the scene. As I conclude this matter I received a transcript from David only a day after his passing. What more proof could I have been given? I now give you his script as I received it.

Script of 2.9.93 *We have located David and brought him to the light. Be patient for other news as he is in recuperation at the moment. He emphasises that it was Ann he always loved! Find a way to pass this on with his regrets of passing in this way but it was for the best. One of the guides here tells of a cerebral haemorrhage with him passing with no pain, the best way out of your world into ours. He also sends his love to his beloved dog Laddie who was always by his side* (then still on the earth plane but who now resides in the spirit world with him receiving all the hugs and kisses that David had stored up for him).

With this script came a personal guidance for me:- *my concern is how you tell her or should you wait for her to ask for help. As it happens the words will come naturally, my point being* NO ONE HAS THE RIGHT TO FORCE AN OPINION, IT MUST BE OF FREE WILL. *My master is calling me now I must go.*

Love to you Lesley we will speak again xxxx

Script of 20.7.93 Mum wasn't well, a little depressed as I was told, as her thoughts had been gathered up by the family and quote *"a message for Gwen not to worry that it's not her time to come here yet, too much to do on the earth plane if she's a mind to"* also *"Dad is not here yet, gallivanting around somewhere, he is always on the go. You know what he is like, he can't stay still for long, and your grandmother sends her love too as she used to communicate with you but has been away for a while. Dad! One of us has gone to fetch him for you; one of us is getting very annoyed with him. One of us is going to get the other one into trouble, one of us is here to serve, the other to play. Do you understand what I am saying? May we also tell you that both you and your daughter have a protector from our world at all times!"*

Dear Reader, this paragraph has more meaning now to me, especially with the insight that the preceding years have given me. Firstly, it seems that in the spiritual realms there is a Universal ruling for certain occasions. When the spirit form reaches their destination they cannot only choose to be at the side of a loved one but also think themselves to a destination, the other side of the world for instance and maybe see some places that it was not possible to do with their earthly existence. Also there are learning places on another spiritual plane and this was where my grandmother was at the time of non-communication. The protector that was talked about I now know is my Gatekeeper Guide, who I use whenever I put pen to paper or when I have to deal with the public when I give a spiritual sitting for them. For instance, a person would come to see me when troubled and I endeavour to, through my spiritual links with their spiritual family, offer some support and encouragement to overcome their dilemma. The purpose of the Gatekeeper is to bring forward the most trustworthy of that family, to speak up for the recipient and keep any other spiritual entities at bay. My words are vetted by my philosopher guide, who works with me and where compassion is needed or healing given my healing guides come to the fore. I am able to see the betterment of mind, body and soul of my recipient as they may have come to me looking as if they have every worry in the world on their shoulders and they quite often go home with a smile and a hug for me which I treasure, and sometimes a loved one says in my ear as my sitter is leaving, give him or her a hug from me, of which I am happy to comply with, then I know it is not all my work that day or hour that has been put aside for the communication with spirit. I would also like to inform you, as I was once told by my spiritual advisors, that everyone has their own three guides from birth and any one of you can start to put them into play at any time of your lives and as your lifetime's pathway opens up, more are assigned to you depending which spiritual direction you are pursuing at the time as the knowledge has to match your vibration and your particular spiritual adviser's vibration for a good connection. Be advised that any misuse of this valuable connection will result in the plug being pulled at any time from either side of the veil, so use it wisely and well to make our time here on earth worth while and a much happier place to live in as we do not know when we may be recalled to where we have come from.

Chapter 2

INTERACTION WITH SPIRIT

Dear Reader, I have chosen this part of the book to highlight happenings through my diary with spirit, where our spiritual family wishes to show they are still interacting with the earth plane, and where possible, some family connections can indeed help with the grieving process both here and in the spiritual realms. Even to include outside personal family links such as friends, are never left out. My first recollection is where my sister Barbara's daughter Tara was to be married, I received several messages on the following scripts:

Script 4.8.93 *A message for Sarra. We know you can communicate with your grandmother; it is a very logical step for you to start here, you have the power for sight so use it well and you will go far, you also have the backing of your future husband as he also has the insight. On this plane we call it having the power of thought so do not be afraid to use it, you are well earthed* (protected) *as you have the temperament to see through danger and automatically shut yourself down! She must believe more in what she is seeing as she is lacking confidence in this, she can teach you then. Sarra is quite happy at work, they will look after her and reward her often! Her talents will stretch to beyond her wildest dreams! I have learned on this plane to be more tolerant. I'm sorry for any hurt I may have caused in the past, I'm truly repentant now! Oh! You understand, thank you, little Sarra is my life. I have seen the photo on the mantle shelf of the two of us, get her to frame this.* (So like her to still want things to be right) *I think her home is full of love and I'll help her to keep it that way! As you had faith in your grandma she can have faith in me on communicating. We know this to be true.*

From the Clan, Mum H XXX

Dear Reader Unfortunately even with the help of spirit, you personally are the one that is master of your own destiny. Now she is happier than ever with her new choice of partner Andrew and her two children by him, presenting me with two beautiful grandchildren whom I adore.

Back to our original **script of 4.8.93** *Little Grandad is here too* (Sarra affectionately called my father her little Grandad) *we know Sarra would like to know that his pocket watch will be worn at Tara's wedding, as a sign of little Grandad's presence, it's a lovely idea, and isn't Brian an old softy to think of it. Grandma also wishes Sarra to wear her necklace when she is bridesmaid to Tara; this would make her happy too. Is everything now ready for Tara's wedding? It's not long, please communicate with me or us, on how things go on the 28th I* (my father) *would love to have been there physically and I think this is what is wrong with your mother at the moment as she is showing signs of depression. She will snap out of it and when this depression passes her health will improve. We are all pleased for you darling, go now in peace and we will communicate another day.*

All our love and blessings for now. Xxxxxxxxxxx

Script of 1.9.93 *Yes we have been waiting for you to get in touch, much excitement here. The wedding was a great success we were all there thanks to you. Dad was pleased about his watch, he was very proud to see Brian and John admire it at Barbara's home it is such a shame he couldn't join in. As a matter of interest the time of the day has no consequence to us, so never be afraid to put pen to paper. On this plane we have a saying our god is just the same, day or night and we know you are there all the time in the same way. One of us is going to fetch Norman* (my father) *one of our healers was there to help heal you which is done better at night when you are resting. Norman is here now but don't keep him long as he is tired* (meaning energy depleted as spirit does not need sleep to keep the ethereal body going as we do in the material body) *Darling, one of the group is going to stay with you for now. He is* *very happy to communicate with you with much love and will, one of us says comfort you when needed, that's all for now.*

God Bless love Grandad, Dad, Mum and all xxxx

P.S. we are only here to comfort or to give guidance not to be trivial. Our job on this plane is to oversee the living to help them where necessary; we believe you are now in good hands with the church. Pursue this field for guidance up to a point, but we can guide you on a more personal level as to where you would like to go from here, our peers of further knowledge guides us, to guide you, do you understand? My mother would like to tell Lil (my father's sister) *that she is not to worry when it is her time to come to this plane we would help her like you did for Norman, so try and visit her when you can! Please don't fail to do this we are counting on you. We thank you very much.*

Dear Reader, my father's sister had for a number of years residing in a home for the elderly and I visited her only at Christmas as a rule, but my cousin kept me informed if she ever fell ill, and through this message I made it known to the staff of the home to ring me if she deteriorated. She actually died in 2002 the same day as the Queen Mother of which I will tell you later. Once again an interaction with the other side of the veil of which I am only too pleased to be of service. So why don't you also give this method of connection a try as it is a natural instinct for our brain waves to communicate even though the material body is not functioning, and think what joy you can give by assisting your spiritual family in this way.

Also from this script I had asked for other methods of communication skills such as real sight instead of sixth sense or hearing spirit but the reply came back: *Our guide can help you, as with the time of Norman's passing with the mind to mind link and the words come quite naturally now you have perfected this way of communication and we think any other way would be wasted.* I was then given a little insight as this script went on *"I'm not of your family, my name is Clarissa, I am an elder and I am able to communicate with you and have permission from your family in spirit. Do you mind?* (I didn't feel uncomfortable with this energy as it builds when I use the pen to each entity that wishes to communicate, so I replied telepathically to continue) *I have the power to communicate quite easily. Relax. See – I came through just the same, we don't have the power to communicate on this plane the same as on yours, we have to wait for you to get in touch or be invited to do so, then every one jumps in on the line similar to your Net meetings on the computer. We are pleased to do this as we know you are quite experienced and keep most of our messages for the right time and place to pass them on. Our lower entities are only here when we are not, do you understand?* "Yes." *We are always close to you and no harm will ever come to you, such as bad spirits entering your body or your home, so dispel these thoughts.*

Back to the **Script of 1.9.93** I was told, *"One of us says any other way is blocked to you so that this talent lives. Your guides need to communicate so that they may go onto a different plane/level like your grandma Goodacre did, do you understand Lesley? Good! Our world is a mirror image of yours but no wickedness for us here! It is safe to live! We have no parallel existence that you could comprehend as we are closer to the higher being, day by day and earthly mortals help us in this quest with their vibrational links."* Yes *"I think that one of us is trying to communicate with me, I am going to see what they want. Hold on there! We are now in control again. We want to know why you originally communicated, is there something wrong?"* Yes. *"Your father was at the church service when you took Gwen (my mother) along. Tell her as we had promised and as we saw all that went on he was allowed to stay all day. We know this will comfort her and didn't she look well! We have been trying very hard on her behalf with her health, so if there are any changes please tell us straight away. Promise! Are you OK he says! We are being told we must go now, please write again."* (Clarissa who is she, I asked as I was given this name at church) *"Yes! We know her, she's a laugh, and you won't* *go far wrong with her. This is Dad speaking! My knowledge of her goes back quite some time. In Ireland when I was a child Clarissa was one of the elderly neighbours who took me under her wing. As I was the youngest of nine children she thought I needed more love. She was a large cuddly lady as I know from one of her many squeezes. One of us has to be there to teach you and she has been chosen for a short while, so don't be afraid of her, we know she can help you with many aspects of spiritual life which may be of interest to you.*

Bye for now from the gang xxxxxx.

P.S. One of us is here at all times for you and any one of us can do this, we have the knowledge to help in this area, our problem is how far to go for any particular person as we know a little learning is a great power. Our power grows with yours, helping us to progress too. We understand that writing is not enough and you wish to experience more but you are at an age where you could be frightened of anything that doesn't come naturally. Do you understand? This will happen at the right time for you to enjoy, so do not be afraid!

Dear Reader, at this point I was so frustrated that Dad hadn't shown himself to me but they definitely had a point of not progressing too quickly. Though even to this day in the year of 2002 I have only had a quick glimpse of a spirit, other than in my sixth sense of a mind to mind link while script writing, or in my dreams or when I link in with meditation. My most urgent need to know of this other sphere we call the spirit realm and their helpers was as I recall when I had had a mild stroke. In desperation, as the right side of my body had been affected, I prayed for the strongest of my healers to come forward and for my gatekeeper guide to protect me from any other forces other than those who would make me well. A truly remarkable thing happened. My powerful Indian guide who had made his presence known to me in the 1990's came so close to me. I saw in my minds eye (which is called your third eye) just one of his eyes, a nose and his mouth as if he was right inside my head, to show he was indeed with me, that close. I will never doubt spirit again. My body recovered within three days. The nursing staff said that they were amazed at my quick recovery as from the brain scan I had indeed had a small bleed.

I was recently taken into hospital for my only experience to date of a major operation. I was naturally very worried of the anaesthetic, so I asked my spirit friends to keep me calm. They produced some wonderful images of my guardian angels as I was wheeled down to theatre. I awoke to discover that I was not in the recovery room but back in the ward and I had distinctly heard a voice saying "she looks so peaceful we will wake her later."

Scripts of 2/3.10.93 started with a sort of nice reprimand: - *We are here and were expecting you. Where have you been? Please try and make this more regular as we are able to teach you more. Our brother is here, "**Michael**" he says not to worry what time of the day it is as we know how difficult it is for you to be on your own in the quiet.* I now know "Michael" as being a higher entity, that of an Archangel. This was pointed out to me in 2005 but I could not take this on board at the time as I now can with hindsight. It was awe inspiring to know that an Archangel would want to be part of my life's teaching. WOW! BRING IT ON!

Dear Reader, at this time my husband did not know I had such a gift and that I needed privacy to let the pen flow with abundance. He would either interrupt or just ridicule, he even at one point asked, after I had chaired a church service, if "the toffee papers floated from the ceiling or tilted tables had transpired?" This was all done with good hearted humour but it is only now in the year 2000, the enlightened age, I'm able to come clean with my spiritual calling. He often exclaims "I let you use our home for your ladies meetings even though I believe when you're dead you're dead, what more do you expect!" He is referring to my awareness group evenings, where in 2002 gentlemen are also attending showing that men have their caring side as well. I just smile and say is your leg playing up dear, would you like some spiritual healing to which he never declines. So spirit must be working on him in a subtle way too. Also, he even asked if he could help when we had a burglary at the church when the P.A. system was stolen and he replaced this with a system from his band days. His help and generosity was invaluable and greatly appreciated. As I recall he gingerly went into the church for the first time, I think he thought that someone, or something, would suddenly jump out at him. He then got rather blasé with the nerves, mounting the rostrum with a jovial display acting like The Reverend Mr. Ian Paisley "Now look here you sinners," in that Irish brogue of his which made me cringe at first then made me smile as I told him there was no such displays at our church and that spiritualism comes from a different way of teaching the Divine Father's pathway. Indeed when one has attended a spiritualist church for some time a wonderful new zest for life begins. One realizes that we are never alone in this world and ones particular charisma that one puts out to others can change their lives causing a knock on effect. Further more to this same script a paragraph said, *"referring to your arthritis, our leader here will not let it get too difficult for you to write, so don't worry, work is in progress, our guide here says the situation will dispel! Good to see you smile, you're welcome, Grandad says you are always a bright girl so don't get so despondent. Our grateful thanks for communicating with us! We haven't a lot to tell you; firstly Norman* (my father) *wants you to know he is here!"* To which I must have thought is dad there? This reply then came back… *"Of course he is and Sarra's Grandma Shepherd too! Lots of love surrounds you, and we now welcome the next guest, David, your next door neighbour says you look wonderful Sexy, only joking give my love to Anne and I'm looking forward to seeing her enjoy life again as I know I was a burden to her! And a naughty boy! But I think she has forgiven me. My only regret is we didn't have longer to make up for lost time. I'm very well here and your family are great. They have made me so welcome! "One of the important things they teach you here is to be patient where contact is concerned."*

To continue on **7.10.93** David came through again with: *David is here for Anne. May I pass this on that I'll always love her, my real love! Remind her of our pleasant afternoon the day I passed over. It was so nice that our friendship was re-kindled; our love had been tested but always true. I send my love to Laddie* (their Border collie). *I have come to terms with this way of life very well and one of these days evidence will be found to show I am around the house all the time, just to comfort you not to scare you. Maybe an ornament moved from its original place."* My thought asked him "when" so that I could prepare Anne but he came back with "*not sure, it takes a lot of energy and also I wouldn't want to worry the family.*"

(GUIDE) *We realize Anne doesn't respond the same as you do to spirit, and it is difficult to get this over to her so please take our kind regards for helping him.*

Your communication has to end! Bye."

THE NEXT EVENING

Yes we are here, that was quick. We are only too pleased to communicate again, such an abrupt end yesterday evening as John had come home! We know it is difficult keeping this secret but he will begin to be curious and help you later on to collate this knowledge.

Dear Reader, this has finally now come to pass as in late 1999 I started to compile this manuscript on to a floppy disc for the PC, and although through many years as a touch typist this part comes easily, my computer knowledge was minimal. I find his expertise brilliant. What wonderful ways spirit has in their working with the mind to mind links of those we love. We only have to ask whether they be in spirit form or here in the now and present.

Script of this same evening read as follows: *May we accept an invitation for tomorrow, it will be great to communicate by speech, we will be there don't worry! Our friends are quite excited to meet you, it will be good. My mother says you are to communicate with us after your church meeting too! Is that OK?* "YES" *My grateful thanks. We must go now. Speak to you tomorrow. All our love Lesley and our fondest regards to the family and Todd the family pet* (a border collie cross with a bad burn scar on his back due to mistreatment) *xxxx My mother says that he has a good life yet for awhile at least, you treat him so well.* In our kingdom animals reign at a higher level than yours as they are born psychics. You are aware of this aren't you; many of us here take quite some time to come to terms with the loss of a pet, as we know you on your earthly plane do. But they all come over to us to start a new beginning here, one of us misses his dear dog Laddie but he knows he will see him and let him reside with him shortly as the impending spirit form will be coming to us soon. Ending with - *My blessings with you dear, you do so much good work, it is Helena speaking. We know of your work with our dearest mortals on the earth plane, go now before you get all emotional over us, no further message tonight, wait till tomorrow, our relations are calling so must go now love.*

Our Best from, The ClanxxxxxxxxxMorexxxxxxxxxDad

Dear Reader, this message implied that I would get a personal message from them through a visiting medium if I was to go to church, the latter being the family dog.

My neighbour's dog, so Ann tells me, has gone to spirit at the time of writing this, thus placing him with his beloved master David living out his spiritual days with a special companion by his side.

THE FOLLOWING DAY

I had indeed received a message from my visit at church but I was perplexed on some information given. Putting pen to paper my script came forward with 12-15 months for a move and that the property market would rise a little ensuring a move to a bungalow that my husband and I had discussed. Then on asking how they could unravel my confusion on the message I had been given *"You were given a bottle of champagne! Oh, we don't know, other than this information would be revealed later. The Ernest and Alf you were given is also a mystery here too. My mother is looking for you! I am sorry darling my son is calling me back to another plane, says your Grandad. The Ernest and Alf is something to do with our family. Going for now and you can ponder. More of us are coming in now. It's early! We don't get going till 12p.m.*

Right, my son is here now so I send my regards to you! We are expecting a visit from our leader, one of us here says it is important information for you and to get this down. Our belief is going well we think there! GOOD! Blessed are those who are touched with spirit. Our teachings are too good to be true! All of this is to enlighten you. Many of us here are bowled over with your communication, I expect you are too! Within such a short time you have perfected this way of communication. Ernest seems to be on your grandmother Goodacres side. A fact of life here is that one always needs someone to communicate with from the earth plane, our fondness for you and your talent is welcome here! Our brother Norman is coming through now! We are looking forward to learning your news. *My love to you dear daughter get Gwen to go to the church again and I promise I'll be there for her! I tried to come through for you to hear my voice but to no avail, I'll persevere and maybe next time? LOVE YOU TOO DARLING! We are handing you over to John's Auntie Helena. Are you alright dear? Our love to you, that is from Lily my sister too. We sent the message through your visiting medium of the bottle of Champagne and Raffles. We thought you would have known the significance of this. It is the trip to Oz that you only dream of at the moment but it will come true and then you will believe that what you are getting with this form of communication is true also.*

One of us says "Believe with all your heart" "You are the chosen one", and "Be wise" "Our guidance is for ever", also "one of us says be careful who you impart the knowledge to as you gather it in. A perfected state here has been proven. For instance, we talk of a newly arisen soul meeting with our Universal laws and the demands that we hold dear on this realm. *Helena says you are still her favourite person, who is next then! One of us is saying Norman gets so uptight if he's not included, one of us say's, BOSSY BOOTS it's just like him.* ("YES" I thought) *As you write our fond memories it holds us there for a short while. One of us says - this is no problem though as we could go on all night, OUR LOVE IS ALWAYS WITH YOU. Our Leader here is ever watchful for misuse of (THE POWER) which would hinder our move on to higher things on other planes and yours on your pathway.*

The next step in your development is to test yourself with someone else's memory. One of us is saying sweeter things than this can come by communication. Our people here are in abundance, our enlightenment is forever, our souls here are misplaced until contact and one of us is pleased that you are a quick learner and with ever the open mind. Incidentally if one of us misleads an earthly bound mortal we are banished from communicating for a while to atone by our spiritual leader. Does this make sense? Your communication has to end!

Farewell and goodbye for now.

From The Clan and your leading light. *XXX* X.

Dear Reader, from these script readings it is shown so perfectly how life on the other side reacts with ours in such a way that you can't help but be inspired once you have tapped into their knowledge, I will show you more as you read on.

Sometimes an abrupt break is necessary if the concentration is broken such as with the entrance of my husband into the bedroom. I find this is the best place to work, in bed with an A4 lined pad propped up against my knees with the bedside lights on this being the most relaxed and comfortable position for me.

Script 26.10.93 *May we just finish our correspondence of 7.10.93. Just to say that we know you wish to gain more knowledge and one of us is here to guide you in this. Our leader is here now! And he will help you. Firstly translate the following then read after our first impressing thought to let you write as we dictate, then next we will print our names of those present. Today they are RACHEL, ROBERT, GERTRUDE ANNIE, AND G.L.C GROUP LEADER (GUIDE) One of us is guiding you.* **OK!** Ordinarily we would only let the words flow while you are in a trance like state, but today one of us is trying to take over your persona and one of us is disciplined enough to know that this is wrong, don't worry, over here it is quite natural for a display like that as to a one to one of a playful nature which is not allowed as far as we are concerned.

The message was to be, *could you help my son to go and visit his mother, and we know you will tell him if the occasion arises, his name is Robert over here and his mother's name is Norma over there. An odd message our leader says but it must be a test. One of us says be brave, there are lots of things planned for your destiny on the earth plane, so much so that one of us will be of service day and night for you.*

We do not need to sustain a material body so this is possible and we are only too pleased to assist you as we know your knowledge grows day by day. Our only aim is to please you! As you progress so do we, thus enabling us to go onto a higher plane to ask for your field of vibration to be lifted. Other people are now tuning into you, ordinarily we do not allow this but there is an urgent message for you to go and see Gwen, tell her that everyone here is helping her with her health, she has a lot of living to do yet. One of us says your ability grows and the next step is near, our aim is to have you close to us for ever, sorry our master is now calling we must go.

Your ever loving family and personal guides xx.

P.S. One day the knowledge of all this will be clear and one day our hearts will beat as one. This plane is overflowing with love and you will never want for it.

Love as always. G. (Grandmother Goodacre) "END"

Script 22.11.93 *We are here, good evening to you darling Lesley, we have been waiting for your contact, thank you for the flowers Mum Shepherd says,* (I had visited her grave and planted some African Violets which were her favourite) *she is in splendid health though she is not here at the moment. Colin* (my brother-in-law) *wants to believe in you, he badly wants to know there is an after life especially as you have just attended his cousins' Maureen's funeral, by the way she is calmer now after her ascension, we are going to help her through her bereavement.* "YES" *we do go through a grieving time also when we pass. Mum Shepherd said she was quite shocked to see her arrive so early in her life, but this is the way sometimes!* Believe us when we tell you, life here is pleasant for those who believe in faith, that our spirit never dies!!! *Bless you dear heart for contacting us, we will not keep you as you seem tired and you need to rest. Before we go Marie's father is here to wish her his best too. We are getting quite a large gathering as time goes on. Our love to all those on your plane from ours, and existing is just that! Grandad says love to you from him. Our leader here says you are coming on in leaps and bounds.* Now is the time to channel your energies to help others as you are fully capable.

Going now love, get some rest.

From, The Clan xxxxxxxx,

X *one special from DAD.*

Dear Reader, as the script above shows I had started to do private sittings to put my helpers and myself to the test, not charging in the beginning until I was so inundated with my time being taken up that it was encroaching on my material life. So if you decide to take the challenge from spirit create a happy medium, (excuse the pun). A reasonable charge for half an hour's work, which in some urgent cases I find is more like an hour, with the need to explain where loved ones are plus a stronger vibrational link from the sitter merging in with mine to their loved ones in spirit thus forged and making an excellent channel. This happens quite frequently now after several years of tuition through my spirit friends and helpers telling me of the wonderful sights that have met them on going over.

I can say with my hand on heart that in the year 2002 as I am writing this part of the manuscript my experiences are still going on with wonderment after wonderment. I am so lucky to have created this strong link which had started unhappily with my family bereavements. I had nine within the space of two years. Some of these were close relatives such as my father and mother-in-law, two cousins in their early forties, and because we have always been a close knit family here on the earth-plane, it stands to reason that we are all going to be just as close on the higher side of life. Why not start your channelling off and enjoy all that I am still enjoying.

Script of 23.11.93 *Hello! Back so soon! We are only here for a chat today. OK what would you like to know?* WHAT IS IT LIKE ON THIS PLANE? *The dimensions on the earth plane are different of those here. In spirit form some of us say it is easier here than on earth as we have a law abiding existence and sweet natured mortals to deal with, yourself included. Dad says he is much more tolerant now than he used to be, your Mum would be pleased to learn. Our guide tells us you have come to terms with this form of communicating as the best way! GOOD! You would be foolish to try any other method, attaining* *such perfection we are able to get in touch with you at ease. The pressure will be on you to use this skill wisely; we also understand that you are now a member of a spiritualist church. Good girl! This is a very good start! We can assist you; just ask at any time, our guide here is very good too! Our blessings are with you dear Lesley on your quest to serve others. Barbara is rather perplexed regarding your mother Gwen. Tell her not to be! Go carefully as she is on a raw edge. Your going away is causing this and she feels she is burdened again! We are doing our best to make Gwen more assertive but it is hard at her age! Ring her.* (I sent the thought message back that I was due to visit her before going on holiday) *Good girl, she would welcome a visit from you. Also good luck with your stall to further the cause of increasing funds, it will be a great success.* (This was in reference to a Christmas Fair which the church committee and myself included, were organizing) *our leader here is proud of you in fact we all are!* (Because of my concern of our travelling to Australia for the first time, some 27hrs of flight at least, this reply was given). *You'll be all right, travel will be easy and when you come back to the grindstone things will become easier you'll see! A happier abode is foreseen living in a bungalow* (with this there were many locations given by different quarters of the family, mainly with a sea location, if not as a main home but a holiday home. I believed nonsense at the time but this was indeed a foresight of things to come quite some years later.) With the script message continuing with, *there are more of us putting our two-penneth in now, you have really started something and we all want to help. One of us says a bungalow by the sea like your Auntie Madge and Uncle George, they love it at Mablethorpe, by the way you must go and see them says Dad. Now, what are we going to do with you! Such frivolity, it gladdens our heart our leader says! Also Grandma Goodacre says what is the mother of the bride going to wear and will you be as radiant as you were the day you came to see Grandad and me on your wedding day. We know about the wedding photo of all four of us that you gaze at to remember us which is part of your collage of Family memorabilia hanging on the wall.* Ending with: *Our leader says you must rest now as it is late, we will come again to you.*

Love from The Clan
Xxxxxx
xxx
x

Dear Reader – please note that the kisses were exactly as my Mother-in-law used to write them on her cards, yet another piece of proof.

Do write everything as it comes in as some parts might be relevant at a later date.

Script 25th & 26th Sept. 1993 *We are here. It is nice to hear from you. We are always pleased to hear from our pupils. Clarissa (CLARA) is present for your guidance and some of the family for a chat. As you have found out Clara is short for Clarissa and she is indeed an aunt but only by name, as she was a good friend of the family living next door to him in Belfast Northern Ireland when your father was little. She used to look after him as he was the youngest of nine children and not getting the attention she thought he should.*

We know of your visit to church but unfortunately we couldn't make another connection with the medium. Let us know of any further visits and we will do our best. Grandma Goodacre here, "One" of us is always with you, my father your great grandfather is also here now and he is saying that your Uncle George and Auntie Madge are not well – please could you ring them. I sent a thought back that I would. *Your father Norman is well and here too, also many others are gathering in your honour. There is no need to ask if he is well as he is always in robust health on this plane. He misses you he says as I communicate this to you from us all. What can we do for your health, that is easy ALL YOU NEED IS FAITH and we can try our best from this world. Lie back when we have finished our communication as we know of someone good in this field to dispel this particular condition.*

Script 29.11.93 *Welcome to you dear Lesley. We are honoured we have a distinguished guest this morning on this plane from yesterday your Majesty. It is nice to hear you laugh for a change. Present here today are Grandad & Grandma Goodacre, Dad and Haide*e (Mum and Dad-in-laws) *and our distinguished guest is your Great Uncle Bert, who is Grandad's brother. He is concerned about Uncle George's health* (Gwen's brother). *One of us is crying for him as his nephew in America is very ill, use Gwen as a Liaison officer to see if we can offer any help.* I said I would pass through the information needed, but as it happened the news didn't filter through until the crisis was over. In the meantime I sent out my healing connections by thought by instinct, as at this time I was not so aware of how powerful the thought for healing was as I am today. *Please give my love to Gwen* (Mum). *And yes I'm fine. You know me, very resilient. God Bless you darling. LOVE YOU! Going now – too emotional for you at the moment when we connect. Please don't cry we will meet some day I promise. Life here is good! You'll see when it's your time. You will not want for anything either. We have noticed Sarra is coming on well as a mediator as long as you teach her to your best ability now! We know of your latest upset with John giving you a hard time. He is an idiot but he will learn! We are bothered with your situation and how you are coping with these outbursts. Take things one day at a time. Your Grandma loves you, and she has ways to make him see sense.*

I do now know that spirit can help situations once known, to plant subliminal messages whilst the recipient is sleeping as this is the time that your inner spirit is more receptive to the higher dimension. My husband being a non-believer, (but hopefully I and my friends in spirit are working on this). Now in the year 2002 my husband and I have been having some strange conversations whilst him being asleep where he has talked as if awake, by answering me when questioned "what was that dear" etc. Also he is now quite intuitive naturally and jokes about the fact quoting "I must be psychic". Something I have for some years joked with him about saying the same thing when I try and help with physical unknown situations coming up. John's Mother signed in but was too emotional to speak, so it was passed on that she would help and to send love to her granddaughter Sarra. Auntie Helena also signed in to pass her love on too.

Dear Reader, I found out through medical advice that the outbursts mentioned were due to John's blood pressure due to his menopausal age and it was easily sorted, we were then able to cope better as a couple. So if your partner is going through a personality change i.e. hormone imbalance either a male or female, take my advice, don't suffer - there is no need for it, seek medical advice before wrecking a perfect partnership or long term relationships.

As my Spirit friends have always told me - think before going onto pastures new that may not have been mapped out for your future. Try and change the here and now to your advantage by listening to your Heart Chakra, that little nagging voice deep inside you, when something is instinctively wrong.

This script finished with *Love to Anne, Laddie, Philip, Julie and Paul on the earth plane.*

P.S. We now have contact. We are all here (Family in Spirit) to help David come through his ordeal of passing and as we know of your friendship with the family we are glad to help him. He is being very brave. This has been difficult for him as he was a little lost and bewildered at first. It was a sudden passing and it takes time to recuperate. Thank you Lesley we are leaving you now, it has been a pleasure.

Love from THE CLAN XXXXXXX
X DAD.

These are just a few instances of the interactions from spirit to earthly connections to show that family ties are still as strong when going over to the other plane of life.

When I first began talking with spirit.

Myself aged 16

and when I was 21.

The following illustrations show many generations or 'The Clan'

My wedding in 1967 – most of those present are in spirit world.

The Goodacres – all are in spirit except for Uncle George (on extreme top left).

Standing beside my father on the left is my Auntie Lilly, his sister.

Grandad Mullan whom I have only seen spiritually until this photograph came to light upon clearing my parents home.

Grandad Goodacre extreme left with his brother and my Great Grandmother.

My Goodacre grandparents.

Bread knife incident (Ouija board).

Left to Right, Back Row – my husband John, myself, brother in-law Brian, my sister Barbara.
Front Row – nephew Craig, daughter Sarra, niece Tara and my son Glen.

Chapter 3

ASTRAL PERCEPTIONS

Dear Reader, whilst you will still find interlaced with this chapter more interactions with spirit you will also find that my scripts start to give a little more of what the afterlife perceptions are.

Later on in the book you will also find snippets given to me from bridging guides of an afterlife from another planetary existence. Their wisdom and knowledge is far greater than ours of HOW OUR PLANET IS TO GROW IN THE NEAR FUTURE.

1994

Script of 16.1.94 *One of us says you wish to move home. May we assist? One of us says it is within our power. Now go to see your vender and tell him to pull out all the stops. He is not working as he should! One of us says there are plenty of buyers out there. You will eventually move and this eases monetary aspects. We still see a bungalow for you on the west side of Hinckley and this will be a happier home.*

Mum seems to be happier these days, don't you think? Your business is slack, don't worry about it. As time passes other work comes your way. We hear you are to do a sitting for a lady called Trudy, she has gone through some turmoil with her boyfriend who is now on this plane; one of us says he would like to contact you for her?

May we assure you that you will be safe. With our guidance you must never be afraid to try darling, you have been given this special gift from your re-birth so you must use it. Just because we are on this plane it does not mean we are unable to feel what you feel. Our longings are just the same here even when choosing a home, it is automatic. We are guided to this place and settled into a communal way of life. We know you wish to learn more, so we are helping to develop your senses to help us and your church. Don't ever feel you are unwelcome as this would make us sad! Your talent needs exploiting for our good. Blend emotional anger and stress with pleasure. Protect your feelings more and you'll not get emotionally hurt. We know this is hard but we have had to learn this too.

Our guide tells us with your communication we will learn both ways. Our plane is both heaven and hell but only in an emotional sense. When people stop contacting and they are perfectly able to do so, we then have no purpose, nothing to strive for, no vibrational uplift, which enables us to move onto a better way of life here i.e. to a higher plane. Our guide here says our time is almost at an end so be good.

Love Dad and Gert. xx

P.S. We know you recognise the last name, she is still looking after you (my grandmother Gertrude Goodacre). *She says your move to a bungalow will be this year and not to get so stressed. Our concern is how quickly do you want things to move?* (I relayed A.S.A.P.) *Fine! We will organise certain events. We are pleased to do so for the many times you have helped us. The last bungalow you looked at will be yours this time no question. However, we can't predict events as you have to make these happen, but your choice will be a happy one. May we finally end with the time difference here differing to yours, so the prediction may be a little out time-wise?*

Hugs and kisses as always.
From the Clan. Xxxxxxxx

Dear Reader At this time I was working with Ann Summers and was finding it increasingly harder to create the necessary parties. Whilst packing my things away messages were being relayed to me for the ladies gathered, making my evenings out longer and longer which was causing concern at home. One such message was for Trudy. She rang me for a personal sitting after attending one of the Ann Summers parties where her Grandfather had tried to pass a message onto her. My first paid reading was born spring boarding me onto a new career.

Referring to the passages above, I was at that time residing in a 4 bedroom executive home which was becoming an ordeal through a long drawn out selling procedure taking several years due to the recession.

The move to the bungalow happened as predicted. I was giving a tutorial circle one evening a week helping others to come to terms with their gifts and earthly tribulations were being sorted by their families in spirit with a direct link. Once again I can't thank my spiritual family enough for keeping me uplifted through an unpleasant period of my life.

Script of 2.3.94 *We understand there is no need for gratitude, to serve you is a pleasure. Barbara* (my sister) *was surprised by the family contacts at your church. May we get in touch again?* (I replied – yes). *You have been in touch with Lilla* (my sisters' mother-in-law who had an operatic singing voice); *she was indeed trying to sing with you at church, your assumptions were correct. My blessings with you dear daughter. Love Dad. Helena also sends her love and Auntie Ethel is here too. If you see Uncle Bob please pass this on. Our many contacts here say WE are very lucky to have a contact always in touch with us as it can be lonely without news from OUR dearly departed, this comes from both worlds don't you think!*

Script of 3.3.94 continued with *There is a lady who wishes to pass a message on to Barbara, only she doesn't know how to put it "Please* *be patient."* YES. *The message is that she rushes around too much, things must slow down for her. We know you are the same and it's impossible to do eh! Our lovely daughters are all impossible to live with at times don't you think. Brian* (her husband) is looking much better, putting on a little weight and things are looking a little better for both of them. *Now you are back with me your spiritual guide. Lilla, Brian's mother had to go! But I'll make sure she gets the verbal message of Barbara and Brian's Silver Wedding coming up, she'll be thrilled. May we serve you long Lesley, and keep in touch; we must close now as the hour is not too conducive!* (I was getting a little tired due to the late hour. A lesson I have since learnt to allow more time when putting pen to paper) *We will give some healing to you as faith in our healing is the best in the world! Love from Mary from the family in spirit.* I asked was she my great grandmother? "*Yes*". (I did some homework on this name and found out she was indeed my Italian great grandmother on my mother's side.)

Dear Reader, I would like to point out that I had to ask my sister Barbara for verification of the name Lilla as I had only known her as Lil, though I did know she had a wonderful Welsh singing voice which used to produce a hushed silence when she used to sing Ava Maria in Welsh. This also proved there are indeed more contacts than I first thought and if you are prompted to try this method of opening up the door to spirit interaction you will learn so much more for yourself. As your guides, along with your family are there for you alone, do find that special inner quiet space to put yourself in and then interact. May I wish you good luck?

Script of 12.3.94 *We are here and so pleased with your contact. May we also say your speaker for tonight was, and still is a good philosopher who hits the nail right on the head. You have been both fortunate in getting the message so clear in the past and making* *light of the benefit coming from such enlightenment or prophesy. We will always endeavour to help in all that you do. Just do it!!!*

It is our pleasure to serve, and to help with your church sermons as such at this present time.

I will end this book with a few revelations of this enlightenment.

At this point my pen started to run out of ink just before a message came through. *Please get another pen. Then. Back again. Can we suggest not using it again. The flow has not been right for some time - too slow for us. Please make sure this doesn't happen again in the future."* So you see they even try to guide me with mundane things which make me think that tapping into this energy of contact will never let me, or you, down. But be prepared for one or two reprimands on the way, kindly meant of course, after all they are only one's extended family and peers.

As I resumed the same script that evening:- *May we further suggest that in helping others you ask them to meditate first before picking up the pen for guiding knowledge, also try to rationalise the whole understanding of how Spirit communication works. Mainly we are always here to guide, our knowledge out weighs any other you may be thinking of at the time of writing any passage. Our time here is limitless and accounts to no one person or entity. We can also come and go as we please and our messages, we hope, may be of a fruitful nature. Rebecca* (my niece) *has a heart of gold and her grandmother and your Mother-in-law Haidee wish to communicate this to her and is it possible to arrange a sitting between the two of them. However you may have to persuade her, as she is shy and apprehensive about a sitting. We feel she has thought of asking you but thinks that it may be awkward with you being her auntie. Maybe you could tell her as she gets older she will gradually lose someone without the pain following as death is only of the body and not of the mind, we know of this do we not. Our bereavement here is much shorter than yours as we have such learned teachers on this plane that instil such confidence as to where we go on from here!* Our teachings are easy to understand. The quicker we learn the quicker it is to progress into a wonderful new cycle of life of an enlightened world. Our mortal life is of such trappings we are held back to a larger degree. Our blessings uphold the Universal Law which is given freely to all those who wish to take in their grasp of learning knowledge which comes from within. Our aim is like a life workshop! Never ending. Our civilisation only starts when we pass over to this world. Please instil this teaching unto others who may want to be guided by you. Your quest is easy!

Impart knowledge and acknowledge
LIFE AFTER DEATH.

Our brothers, sisters, mothers, fathers, in fact all relations are back ups to an inner knowledge shared by mankind. Our gospels are the same as the scriptures and many men wish to exploit us but we will fight them. The same as in your daily lives on the earth plane, anyone wishing to exploit you or your kin, you fight tooth and claw for justice. Willing or not, the reference to claw rather than nail brings the animal kingdom into this piece of philosophy. Goodnight Darling, Dad says he'll chat some other time as you have become weary also Helena sends her love too, going now.

ALL OUR LOVE. Xxxxxxxxxxxxxxxxxxx M.
(Munchien - my bridging Guide)
THE CLAN

Dear Reader, I arranged a sitting with Rebecca and it went really well. She had not only started her pathway forward where she eventually went back-packing around Australia, an experience and a valuable memory for her on her learning curve of life. Rebecca missed not only Haidee in spirit but also her other grandmother which came out within the sitting. I'm sure I was able to give some evidence of survival which helped her not to feel quite so alone, as although her parents had split up in her early childhood she had come to rely on her grand parents for the closeness that only a close knit family can bring, and I'm sure going by the many sittings I have performed up to this year of 2003 many have come to me for the same guidance for the same reason. My aim with this book is to enlighten and encourage many of you to take up the challenge, to reconnect with your spiritual families to heal the heartache making you a stronger individual, rather than a person just aimlessly going through life without experiencing it.

I feel that we only get out of life that which we are enduring this time around, the superb effort of living to our up-most potential, ensuring that when more lives are to be lived we have learnt valuable lessons not to be repeated yet again in the future. Let's make our world a better place by starting with our own life's experiences shared in a more positive way towards others, not only in our family environment but towards our friends, who I might add we choose and we have to try harder with family who we have inherited and who need a more careful approach.

The next scripts turn out to be a perception on astral life and interconnection to the earth plain.

Scripts of 28th and 29th March 1994

Welcome, Lesley this is an honour, we have been waiting for a contact from you for some time. Our leader here was a little concerned you had found another method of communication. (I was trying other methods of communication at this time but reverted back to the one I knew well and relayed this to them, to which the reply came) *Bless you! Our wish is that you keep this form of communication and we will assist you.* (I had put the thought out that in the future I would like to publish with their permission, the scripts they have kindly given to me to help others.) *YES! Most definitely we would be honoured to serve in this way; this is what it's all about and why we have chosen you for this form of clairvoyance. Our main method of learning here is communicating with others of peace and love and our knowledge is growing all the time. Our belonging is here for the moment, although one of us is going to pass onto a different level soon, all because of his help with you and he says to thank you. It happens to be your Grandad Goodacre who will now be able to ascend to be with your Grandma Goodacre "Great Reunion." He sends his blessing and says we have had a great time together but now that your dad Norman is here there is no need for him now! My dearest! One of us says don't be sad as he will see you one day! One of us here now wishes to speak to you, only a little shy, it is auntie Ethel and wishes to send her very best of love to Uncle Bob on the earth plane, he is not well and if you have time please try and go and see him. May we continue with an insight to life here? It is similar as your earth plane trees, flowers, birds and pets of all descriptions, our plane here is whatever you wish to make it, our dearest desires usually come to fruition. With an even temperature and a sense of light that does not diminish as the earth plane does which distinguishes day and night. One of us says there are to be great times ahead for you and we are to be part of it. Your medium ship is now to be expanded onto a tutorial field, your training has started. It is a great pleasure to serve in this way. Our aim is to see you part of our little therapy group here in spirit world when it is your time to ascend to us, you have a jovial nature we badly need* (Norman) *dad say's. Auntie Gladys is here, we know you wish her well she has had a little bit of a lonely time till she joined our happy throng. One of us here is wondering how you know her* (I sent the thought back that she belongs to the Shepherd Family, in fact John's Aunt). *Our Blessings go to you dear Daughter and grand-daughter as we leave you, we must close now as our tutor is here. Until we contact again* (make it soon) *maybe even a sighting, Dad is still working on this.*

God Bless, From the Clan xxzxxxxxxx
Xxxxxx
Xx X Mum. S.

Dear Reader, the reference to Auntie Gladys and her loneliness I have been made to understand that although she would have been helped into the spirit realm by a member of her family she craved the bubbliness that the Mullan family and their gathering could give her and to this day she is still giving her input through the clan's messages.

Script of 17.7.94 *We are here Lesley, couldn't wait to hear from you again, our aim is to please you and our blessings too. One of us says how about it then you sexy thing? Another says too much frivolity. We are sorry to hear that Evelyn, Jess's new partner, is quite poorly and will not be long on your plane with only a little time to spend with him. Our leader says when her time comes you are not to worry as she will be expected to pass over quite peacefully. Jess will miss her but he has good friends and relations to see him through. I'm afraid with the best will in the world Lesley, even with this realm's help of healing it is her time as she has become too frail to carry on and it would be a blessing. Before we go we would like to pass a message to John's Auntie Nell, from her husband Bill in spirit as he was allowed to be present at Tara's Wedding. He saw the joy in Nell's face as she remembered him as Tara took her vows. Bill grasped the thought at that moment and it made him very happy with a personal vow to be there for Nell when it is her time, not for awhile yet though.* (I would like to add that Nell is still with us now in 2009) *We would like to end with a wish for a grand-child for you. He will be perfect, the image of the child you couldn't have, do you understand?*

Dear Reader That last paragraph meant so much to me as there was an unborn child that I knew in my heart of hearts would be presented to me once again. I will hold and I know that I will be given a second chance of a very special bond only a mother can feel and that I would gladly wait for that moment to be as a fond grandmother. Indeed some years later Sarra and her hubby Andrew presented me not only with a very knowing grandson, but an angelic grand daughter too, both in the same year. How about that for a promise from spirit, I can also relay that I was so moved I asked spirit for something to mark the occasion to which I received a lovely poem that (set out below) this actually got chosen from many others to be published. All this set me on the road to thinking of printing this manuscript, for you.

FOR EVERY PARENT

The birth of a child is a gift of God
Drawing the ties of love and bondage between families.
To kiss each finger and toe,
That has made this a perfect child
Is a delight every mother knows.
To stroke the candy floss of hair on it's perfect head,
And to hold close such a perfect form of his or her making
Is the largest blessing anyone could bestow.
May the happiness of this moment last for ever.

AMEN.

"A TRIBUTE I WILL ALWAYS TREASURE
TO AIM'E MY FIRST GRANDCHILD BORN"

This was also a spur given to me by my spiritual peers and it taught them that whatever they chose to transcribe to me I will try to help others with the intended knowledge or to bring comfort at that particular time meant for me, with the hope of filling some kind of gap or need that conventional means can't bring.

Script of 19.7.94 *We are all here to welcome our darling Lesley and we were all present at your spiritual church tonight. We had thought our Norman* (DAD) *was to represent us. I'm afraid he got a little tongue tied and well overcome by the situation, but we knew you would contact us afterwards anyway. Were you pleased with the contact through your visiting medium? Your man tonight was quite good but didn't interpret too well as we knew we had communicated quite clearly though Lesley. Our leader here say's are you ready yet, as we have knowledge of you becoming quite clairvoyant, but please be careful of going out of our circle just yet as we vet all your spiritual connections first. Also don't try so hard. As you relax we can alter our vibrations to match yours much easier to help your natural progression. Our mood here is very easy going; we expect nothing and get everything! Pleasure is more of the flesh on the earth plane. Here it is much more of a spiritual nature with feelings much deeper. We get high on perfecting our communication skills. Some of us wait many years to do what you and your family have achieved over a short time as it has been said this evening among the peers on this realm. Our guest list here seems to be getting longer. You may not understand this but we have to take it in turns to communicate with you, aren't you the lucky one!*

Our blessings of course to all of you there. Our leader here says' there is no hurry tonight. (This comment is made quite regularly where spirit ask before encroaching upon your time) *Wonderful! Then here are the messages for you. Haidee* (John's mother) *wishes you all well! Also Evelyn will be fine for awhile yet and to tell Jess not to worry! He loves her so. One of us says maybe he will one day tell you of this and be drawn along a similar pathway as yours as we know many couples who have started in this way.*

Love again from our little clan. Xxxx

Dear Reader, you and your spiritual family wait to blossom and grow. It is so easy to get started. All it takes is a little faith in your sixth sense that we all have, it's just a case of using it to the fullest advantage.

This shows that although Evelyn was Jess's (Dad Shepherd's) girlfriend whom he loved dearly for a short while after the passing of his wife Haidee who was a friend to both of them. Haidee has never shown any animosity towards him carrying on life and indeed enjoying it to the full, as she is no doubt doing the same on the plane that she has found herself on. She informed me that she was finding true happiness on the higher side of life with another. Towards the latter end of her earthly life marriage was a little difficult but that she would still welcome him to spirit world unless of course he chooses another. This would have caused maybe a little pain within our earthly family so I kept this to myself till now, and I say good luck to her too! Unfortunately Evelyn passed to spirit with cancer, and has been sorely missed for her lovely disposition and I personally have come to love the geraniums she gave me which were propagated in her lean-to. I have found that of all the plants, this species thrives over all odds of neglect and you still get a wonderful bloom of colour. Mine are that lovely fuchsia shade which uplifts and brightens the dullest of days much like the lady herself. Dad of course, showed his resilience and after a mourning period and vowing he would never find another to take her place, he has found a new love in his life. Even though in his eighties and his eyesight was failing and the car had to go we still had to phone him before visiting (even in 2003) as he was so busy with his new life style.

Mum conveyed that although my husband John showed no interest at the time of any communications of this nature she said she often caught his thought pattern where he had communicated without him knowing, and also conveyed the wish for direct contact which she knows may take many years but she dearly wishes for it to happen. She knows though that he has to overcome the fear of just knowing that spirit is all around you when you need them and that you have only to reach out for them. Also it is a two way thing, a comfort shared and all that.

Script of 26.8.94 *We are here Lesley. It has taken some time for you to get comfortable. Let us help with your condition as we speak. Our blessings go to all on your plane. We know of the help and guidance you are giving Sarra with the communication from her guide White Feather. Did she ever doubt her connection with this world of spirit? One of us says she has great talent artistically and we know she will reap benefit not only monetary but spiritually from this. She gives endless joy with her special spiritual artistry of long lost pets where her gift shines through.*

We feel that with your impending move you have become unwell with your asthma due to stress, so let us take the burden off you by monitoring your thoughts and helping to move things along more swiftly as we know of your dilemmas before they even take place. Your healing guide is here now with you if you would like to take a break for some healing.

Speak to you soon Love the Clan. xxxxxxxxxxx

I reconnected the same day with more family connections:
One of us here says you wonder whether a trip with Gwen, your mother, yourself and your sister Barbara to Ibiza would be beneficial to all, but as Gwen is so frail would the strain be too much for her? Well the answer is definitely go ahead as it would be a memory for her for the rest of her life. Dad say's he is envious as he has not flown in the usual sense since the war! Mum will surely enjoy the trip and we know when her time is due, and it is NOT NOW. My many followers here say we can always tell when a case is hopeless and in your mother's case although frail, this is not so. Our blessings are with her every day and always will be even

when she goes on holiday so that we can make her stronger for the trip. So don't worry! You girls enjoy every moment and God bless! You all need this special bonding at this time. A word of caution though, you have a testing time coming up with some torment blocking your progress. You are to please yourself more dear, take more of the teachings we have to offer from here, as when it is your time to pass over to us we are hoping you will become a teacher of guidance from this plane too.

We can see eventually you residing in a large abode with many different peoples around you where you will be able to teach others in a different country, but the choice must be yours of when and how.

Dear Reader, as I relay the next script to you please note that quite some time had passed, but to spirit they followed on as if the next day.

Script of 4.9.94 *We are here, Dad's delighted for the contact, he knew you wouldn't let him down he is aware of the holiday planned. We have decided to help in your little adventure so that no harm will come to you. You will all be able to enjoy yourselves to the full including Gwen, she is so looking forward to this. We are aware of her thoughts so we will make sure she is good and ready. Girls all together we hear, you will need a good guardian and Dad has offered, certainly, he is ooh so excited. He doesn't get many calls of this nature, yet.*

Love the Clan. XXX

Script 9.9.94 *Hello Lesley nice to hear from you again, Dad was aware you were trying to contact him on his birthday* (earthly one) *we celebrate up here the time of re-visiting this plane. Our leader here says not to worry, Mum will be quite fit and able to travel, the flight will thrill her and she will remember it till the end of her days. She stays in that house of hers far too much. Dad's OK and in robust health in fact, he also knows you are often too busy to* *contact him on a more regular basis, but be does so look forward to it. Haidee is here too and eager to speak with you. She says not to forget her as her sons always do! Oh! We see they do not wish to contact. Well that makes it difficult. Alright, she says tell them she loves them both, and if possible add to that she often watches over them and loves the contact she is often making to Sarra. She makes her home glow with the love she puts into it with her own decorations and adornment.*

Oh dear Lesley, you are not well yourself are you. I wish I was able to help but we are not allowed back to earth yet, we have to wait here till the time comes. One of us here says that in time you will visit us here. By the way we were aware of you driving a little too fast around that bend today; please slow down with every aspects of your life as we do not want you here too soon. Our leader tells us you have a charmed life and we have been given the job to protect you, you certainly keep us on our toes. Well darling another page is filled and it is time to go.

All our love to you from
Haidee and The Clan or half of it at least? xxxxxxxxxxxxx

Dear Reader, this script indeed was very prophetic as mum is now in 2003 but losing her short term memories but the holiday in Ibiza and that flight she often reminds us of with a fond twinkle in her eyes. The Spanish are very homely people and they made such a fuss of her. When we wheeled her into a local restaurant that we visited often, the proprietor would say to us as we entered Oh! It's Mama and her two gorgeous bambinas and as we were all getting on a bit we would all puff up with pride and have a good laugh.

Please note as a reference to an insight into Astral Law plus I having made many visits to the astral world through meditation along with some very vivid dreams, which some people call astral flight, I am inclined to believe that our inner spirit can take flight whenever the body is relaxed enough, and we sometimes remember them to our delight, so always keep a record of such moments as these. I also believe that spirit can make us take a different direction on our earthly lives through heeding them. If only we have the guts to follow our dreams to a conclusion! Finally I might add that through the years that followed this script I have tried to make my life more varied and my husband will be the first to admit that our lives have never been dull as putting your dreams into action can be fun!

CHAPTER 4

TEACHINGS AND GUIDANCE

Script of 18.11.94 *It is so nice to hear from you even though it is your morning time; we should try this more often as we can spend a little more time with you. It is immaterial what time of day it is as we have no general night or day, and we are only too pleased with the contact which is our main concern. Your teacher today is M. How far do you wish to progress with your spiritual pathway? We know you are more than ready for expansion in this area. May we visit you on a spiritual seeing level just to see how you would react; bearing in mind that this form of channelling is a definite gift for you and it has been given for a working tool for you to help others so please use it.*

Dear Reader, at this point I was given my first experience of reaching higher levels. With this particular guide working with me I was told to hold the pen more relaxed and I remember a lighter feeling when the vibrational energy changed, ending with a rather emotional moment where a denser lower energy came in from my father with: *Oh! My darling I new you wouldn't forget your dear old dad! We have always been close. Is Gwen better? We know! This can be done!* (HEALING) *I'm afraid as I am coming quite close to you as you write you can feel more emotion than usual so don't start me off. Oh good! We know you are good at this that is why! One of us is taking over for now as your dad is quite overcome by it all, we will pass on your love, you are his precious daughter and he will always take care of you, now then, we don't want to upset you further so we suggest that we come to a close for today.*

God Bless and love to you from The CLAN!!! Xxxxxxxxxxxx

Followed by a script to mark the passing of Evelyn:

Hi Lesley we have waited so long for contact, where have you been? Such excitement love as Evelyn arrived into our happy throng. We were of course expecting her; we know you will grieve for her but she really is in capable hands. Our blessings to all families on your plane, and our guide and leader here says well done in matching up with her vibrations, one of us says you probably didn't even know you had! We are conscious of wrong doings in our world as well such as darker elements of spirit. You have qualities above this. Our BEING ON EARTH IS ONLY PART OF THE PATHWAY OF LIFE and YES our knowledge is given freely from where we are now. Mental images of past and present are with us all the time. You have excellent ones. Because life is so short on your earth plane we come to neglect those who pass over. We are not telling you off as you keep in regular touch but others, who may not exercise this ability, though quite capable, cause their spiritual families unnecessary longings to be able to be contactable. For instance your Dad has a strong communicational skill now. I'm sorry that we are waffling but we are waiting for a contact with Evelyn she is in the recuperating area at the moment. She came to us quite peacefully. Look out for miss-spelling its Grandad doing this contact. Oh you are aware of it! Good! Well my girl we are to go quite soon and let you get on with life as you know it. As we prepare a grand reception for a dear friend of Haidee's (There is no animosity). *She helped dad overcome a very unpleasant time in his life "who" is going to help over the next coming years ahead. You look after him won't you darling! Good girl.*

Give him all our love and tell him Evelyn is in the greatest of care at the moment. If he'll go to your spiritual church we will help with a personal communication.

God Bless you darling Lesley.
Your Holy Servant and leader and The Family over here.
Xxxxxxxxx

Script of 19.11.94

Hello Darling. Sorry we only have a little gathering tonight to greet you, so here goes. Dad says he is first, surprise! Surprise! It's about time you typed his poem up. The one you found in his wardrobe when you cleared his things out, he is so thrilled you have displayed it at church. God Bless says Evelyn and how is Jess coping. Oh! She's blubbering now! She needs to know how Bobby was with him too! (I sent my thoughts that they were both coping with her passing and that the two of them were inseparable and Bobby was a little white cairn terrier). *Just as you on the earth plane wish to know that family are alright in a situation like this so does she here in spirit world. Your dad says life on this side is more bearable with you around, and that it has opened a whole new experience for him. Our leader says we must go as you must get a boost from our wonderful healer with us at present and he wants to get started, could you please relax and let us go to work.*

Goodnight Darling and God Bless
From us all present tonight, Dad, E, G, M and
Especially your friend with us
T.xxxxx

1995

Script of 1.1.95 *Hello Darling welcome to our little fold again, we are most honoured you have found the time as we know it is limited. We wish you a Happy New Year to you too; we are all well and wish you good tidings. Our stay up here is very pleasant at this time and we celebrate just the same as you do on the earthly plane, we know you are enjoying yourselves as from time to time we are privileged to get glimpses of things happening in your world.*

Our leader says you have great things in store for 1995 our guidance is crucial although, because of matters taken out of our hands we are unable to part with much information just yet but soon things will be clearer on your outlook. John will be settled for some time and things will look better. YES! Better than you think. Your health suffers because you worry too much; let us do that for you! Be pleased with your achievements as we know you are forever capable but please make certain of the facts with us first before plunging into another aspect of your future as we often know the best route. Follow your feelings to the up-most when they are strong Oh! And by the way, Tara (my sister's daughter) *will have a boy and it will be healthy and, Yes! You will get your bungalow eventually. Please don't overburden yourself with too many commitments as Church Secretary on your church committee.* (This was in fact given to me a little premature as this happened in 1997) *Blessings to you as we leave and also to tell you that we are nicely gathered here now because you are so popular, we know this pleases you. But you are tired and we do not wish to overtax you so we will gather another day. OK! Bless you my child and do be careful.*

Bye Darling Love The Clan.
Xxxxxxxxxxxxxxx

Script of 7.2.95 *Hello darling it is very pleasant to hear from you again, we have been gathering for some time to hear your news if any. Our blessings as always are with you sweetheart. May we say your healing is coming on and your abilities are getting stronger? Our guide here tells us you are destined for greater things than even you can contemplate; our being here is excelled with your stronger power, because we are enfolded into your knowledge all is possible. Our blended pleasure is yours!*

We know of your complications in your world and this has to be overcome and with our help your transition will be painless when your time comes. All our guides here are along with you on this and whichever path you take we will be there beside you. Our dear Lesley, you know we give you the very best of help at all times and we will try not to let you down darling. Dad says if you go to India he will go with you as he is looking forward to this. Mum would be OK wherever you go abroad, so don't worry about anybody you may leave behind. They are in good hands Sarra can help there!

After all three years is not a long time darling and the valuable experience is quite something so go along with the flow!!! See how it pans out. Everything will be made ready when things start to slot into place at a faster rate. Then hasten to your destiny and be kind to yourself for once instead of having a punishing schedule. NO! You won't be bored, far from it! Because we love you we also want the best for you, our kindred spirit, we will always be just a thought away beloved. You asked about animals adapting to new situations as your dog Todd on the earth plane will have to eventually be given to a new owner. We have found that animals easily forget their environment even when they inevitably pass over to us we see how quickly they adapt and we try to reunite them with their owners in this world. Your Dad says he'll adapt and when it's his time to pass over he will look after him and it would be a playmate for Ginger, also a few other pets he has acquired of whom one day you will see.

Goodnight Darling Love The Clan. Xxxxxxxxxx X

Script of 16.2.95 *Hello! Darling we are gathered as usual on this festive occasion, Valentine's week. Our blessings go to you dear, there is no other who contacts so readily and enjoys her work as you do. Be our guide for awhile as we contemplate your further existence. We know of your new adventure and we are behind you in this. Please bless us with more writings as you explore your earthbound world. Our leader says we are quite poetic tonight. Our higher plane is to FURTHER humanity NOT TO DESTROY IT. You will see such abject poverty out in India if you do go. We are not to presume things, our leader here says, as your pathway and destiny has to be yours alone to make the right decision as you see fit but being the kind of person you are you thrive on and need a challenge in life, and there will be plenty of those. So, go for it, as you are blessed with a charmed life, whatever chances you deem to take in life. Our thoughts of course will always be there to guide you and no doubt you will listen occasionally. Our brother here says, is he welcome to join us? We can vouch for him darling or we* *wouldn't ask. Because of the nature of his visit to us, he says is it possible to contact you with a thought. He cannot communicate as you would wish but we will relay his message for you.*

YOUR GUIDING SPIRIT IS A LIGHT FOR US ALL AND HE SAYS HE KNOWS OF YOUR ABILITY TO COMMUNICATE IN THIS WAY AS AN EASY GUIDE TO TELL US WHAT WE WANT TO KNOW. YOUR PLANET IS TO BE RENEWED FOR WE KNOW OF THIS; OUR LEADER SAYS OUR FAITH IS FOR EVER GROWING. "BECAUSE WE CARE TOO!!!"

God Bless and love you always,
THE CLAN
XXXXXXXXXX M. (Munchien)

Dear Reader, this was my first connection with another planetary system's guide of which I will tell you more as you read on. This was also relayed to me by my first bridging guide of whom I am now in regular contact as our world is constantly changing with our universe constantly evolving. Also this is no surprise for this connection to come forward into my script writings as my father and I used to regularly go out into the garden for him to show me the different constellations of stars in the sky. I remember that PG TIPS or BROOK BOND Tea did a series of cards to collect which I diligently saved pasting them into a scrapbook but one day I took them into school for a science project and they were never seen again.

The above scripts also referred to a move with my husband's career enabling us to live in India for a time, which, I might add didn't come to fruition due to his health. The company said it was not prepared to overlook his arterial condition due to the practicalities of health services in that country. This message I have since taken on board due to our impending emigration to Spain as I write in the year 2003, with all the same worries of which I was gratefully given the answers to in 1995. I might add after having an afternoon nap

I had an overwhelming urge to put down some more manuscript as I had let it rest for some time and lo and behold the answers to my questions yet again were spelt out to me through re-reading the above script. If I had not written that afternoon I wouldn't have received some timely instant healing of thought and mind whilst going ahead with the biggest decision of my life, going forward into the unknown with a different culture. My new chosen way of life was to be on a mountain with just over a hundred people in the community where I will have to make my mark. Not to mention living in a caravan for some months before the Log Cabin is built, and all at a later time of life (in my fifties). I felt it's now or never. I decided to put my spirit connections to the test to look after my husband and I to keep things moving smoothly within this transition to a new life. Dauntingly I undertook the endeavour of making new friends and leaving many behind of long years standing, including the many clients I had who regularly kept in touch and to whom I hope will buy and read this book, after all it is mainly due to them that I am writing this book in the first place, to give hope and understanding to an ongoing theme to life ever after.

A post script to this in September of 2004 a change of plan suddenly took place where the non build of the cabin causing quite a heartache led us to take possession of a home some 7 kilometres from my beloved sea shore and incidentally closer to the caravan site where we had been living on for the past eleven months. Because of a further delay by our cabin builders of some two years (which was not acceptable) we found my first instinct of living down in Puerto De Mazarron where the camp site was situated rather than 70 miles inland where the cabin was to be erected, came to fruition and a better pathway leading us forward to enriching our lives beyond compare.

Script of 14.2.95 *Hello darling, this is a surprise! It is so late – couldn't you sleep? Oh well, we can fill your time. At present we have only a few here but more will flock around us no doubt with your contact here.*

Firstly some family contacts. One of us here says God Bless, and Evelyn enquires after Jess's health, great things are ahead for you and we will be sharing in your success. Our leader here says it is an honour to bestow on you the gift of clairvoyance but we are always concerned as to how you will cope with it and how much to give you at any given time. Our knowledge is very limited, as family members we have to ask our peers/your guides, one of us here says it's a doddle "DAD?" YES! You guessed. Our leader says he's the cheeky one here! Where ever you are around the globe you can count on your family ties in spirit to still continue to be of service. One of us say's you are tiring so we will leave you for tonight. Please contact us again darling as you are always welcome.

Love from The Clan.

Xxxxxx

Dad.X.

Dear Reader, this is only a small portion of the love and concern of my earthbound family's wellbeing of which I am always made aware of, on every connection made.

Script of 22.2.95 *Hello Darling it's been a little time with no contact. We have been exploring the possibilities of you going to India and Dad said you would like it there in peace time. He would volunteer to be your punka-walla referring to his days spent in Burma out there. It's nice to see you smile and your laughter is good for everyone. Here from this plane we see such sadness, it is a shame that people view coming over to this veil of life so painfully. Our guide here says there should be no fear of death, as when it comes, it is a natural progression into another way of life. Dad says you would take to it like a duck to water as you have the ability to get on with whatever is thrown your way!*

Our leader here says, not many people grasp the metal, to branch out in giving the wisdom of this world to others as this is a certain comfort and you will be greatly rewarded. Also God Bless you darling, what an achievement today has been for you. We were with you in the hall of remembrance of John's 25 years at his work place. Our guide here says not many of us achieved that at one firm. Our guide here says maybe you will achieve the same in the clairvoyance field. We are carefully priming you to do just this due to you being well blessed with goodness towards your fellow man/woman. My sweet child you are the only person we would wish the very best of all good fortune on. Our love as always and you are forever in our keeping and great things will be yours. We commend to you great accolades from our best teachers here of great understanding and dealings of your earth plane. First, before ascending to our wonderful way of life on this plane be aware of the bigotry amongst your so called spiritual friends.

You are contacting us at a very prestigious moment as some of us are going onto a higher plane of afterlife and may not be able to be contactable for sometime. Don't worry, it is our way here. You have helped in their progression, do you understand? NO! *Well it is to do with the vibrational energy link of the spiritual contact which grows stronger every time we link up which goes both ways so that your Psychic/Clairvoyance ability will also grow along with us. Maybe even the ability to see us, as at present if you blink you would miss us; it is this quick at first. It may not be your fault it may just be that we have not perfected the art to do so together. You will always sense us around you, just like you usually do; we give you this as knowledge, which is a wonderful thing, but are you brave enough to experience it?*

God Bless you once again from us all at our own little haven of this heavenly world.

Yours truly,
The Clan.
Xxxxxx
& Lil.

Script of 26.2.95 *Hello dear, sorry you couldn't stay with us due to your ill health yesterday, let's see if we can cheer you up today with some news. Our leader here for instance says to be patient* *and the good times will be with you sooner than you think. As you start off on a different approach to life career wise, our knowledge on this is limited at the moment, only to say that you will be more at one with yourself and you'll not want for anything. This is well overdue as you had been unhappy in your vocation for some time and we are thrilled that you are to take a spiritual pathway with your career at this present time. You are a hard worker in all that you do and your achievements are always noticed by those around you, also your healing will come on in leaps and bounds not only for yourself, but to give to others too.*

Development must go on Grandad says and that he is so proud of you, his little prodigy he adds. He suggested you for this given pathway on our plane of existence here. We know nothing of your tremors of life as the pace of life moves much quicker in this dimension with goodness begetting goodness. One of us says he remembers when the entire world was in turmoil but things are improving gradually with fellow man helping others to cope with their lot. Our faith is forever with you to do the right thing at the right time; something we will not forget is your input. Be kind to yourself more and stop worrying about others, they will always do whatever they want to do anyway!

Our aim is to give you peace of mind to do good things to benefit your aims in life while endeavouring to give us as much contact for many a long year and maybe even with John's blessing eventually as he is becoming quite psychic and he will in time, come to terms with it just as you have done. We would like also to pass on that we have discussed that one day you will meet us here in this world and become a teacher much respected, allowing you to be yourself instead of what you think others want you to be.

We will now take our leave so that we can administer some healing much required as soon as your pen is at rest. God Bless and sleep well, rest assured we will always be at your side to help you through.

Your devoted parents of the past and the future.

THE CLAN.XXX

And a special hug from Dad "you need them" x.

Script of 1.3.95 *Hello darling we are all gathered for you. We were with you this afternoon at your spiritual church and we thought your medium friend Diane using the ribbons was a delightful way of communicating and the congregation enjoyed it as much as we did she did it so well. Your efforts will soon shine, my sweet child, you are an inspiration to others, so long may it continue. We are all blessed with humour but not many show it as freely as you do. When it is your time to meet us here you will be so welcomed, our beneficiary of spirit here says what an honour, your guiding light is always so bright and many will want to follow you.*

Blessings go out to all the family, at this present time, because you need it so we place a golden rainbow over you and a calm sea.

Our leader here has many profound sayings don't you think, may we give you some of our philosophies from time to time? Thank you!

Firstly you ask for some insight of the way of life here. Well, our childhood sweethearts also reside here along with all our lovers, husbands and wives as we are more than able to live in harmony which would be unthinkable on the earth plane and we understand that forgiveness is our virtue. This fortifies us and nourishes our enhancement of enlightenment which enables us to go on to better things. You will have learnt much of this on your earth plane before reaching us here and your progression will be speedier. Do you understand? I know you do (butts in Grandad) as *we have communicated for some years. Our bearing on this message is that you can never learn too much and the help you give to others on the way only serves to better yourself. One of us says that only the other night another mortal came to our world so bewildered that it took us several days to calm him down and as you may or may not know, a state of shock and disbelief on the passing is sometimes very hard to bear, but as you have kept this line open to us this would not be so in your case. Our leader here says we must do our chores now so we would like to take our leave of you with these thoughts and we will always be of service. Goodnight Darling,*

From all the clan, especially Dad and Grandad,

Love and Hugs as always xxxxxx

Xxxx

XxM. (Munchien)

Dear Reader, I do hope you have found this last passage as enlightening as I found it and it's so gratifying that we still have a format of life in spirit world that enriches one's existence. As I have found out through meditations (privately, and sometimes in a group situation), I have progressed to where I am today. I have been given the privilege of seeing the Halls of Learning so if one chooses you can learn so much more than here on the earth plane, this of course is only my opinion.

Why not try and experience this for yourselves. You only have to find some pleasant drifty music and reel the tape or disc on till it is approximately 30 minutes toward the end, then close your eyes and think of someone in spirit that you love. Ask them to take you along a sandy beach and imagine that you are holding their hand as you walk along. Visualise footprints in the wet sand appearing in front of you, these are your protective, spiritual guiding forces that are leading you to where your loved ones reside. You may just want to sit awhile with them to talk, and as you talk just breathe in their favourite perfume or after shave that they used to wear as they come close. When the tape clicks off this sound usually jolts you back to the present. Write your experiences down as they may make some sense to you later, especially if the moment is of comfort or you want their guidance through a difficult patch of your life. Don't forget nothing ventured, nothing gained. I might add as you go about your daily business you may smell this fragrance again and just know that your loved one is with you whatever happens.

Script of 10.3.95 *Hello darling. Sorry to hear your news regarding John's health. You wish to know how serious! Oh! We see your dilemma. It changes things with the job situation in India. Dad's here and he is so sorry, we will of course help as much as we can. Concerning his arterial problem we could try and dispel this blockage with your help and guidance as to where it is.* "YES" *We will be of assistance to you darling every day counts and we do not wish him to suffer like your father. Whenever the need arises we will be there with our healing vibrations to give through you. We hope this has eased your concern darling, we are always with you, just ask for our help, anytime.*

God Bless and love to you from your everlasting friends in spirit
From this plane to yours
THE CLAN XXXXX

Dear Reader, as you can see from the above script, I was really a novice at giving healing from the spirit realm. At this time John eventually had to succumb to several arterial operations including a pioneering operation in 2003 where a false main artery was fitted at the aorta in the neck to the groin. With the help of my healing guides at times keeping the pain at bay, he is now a new man. You must never rely on your healing gift alone whether it is to be given or received, get the malady backed up by the medical profession, even if it is just to check how things are progressing with your health. You never know, you may be surprised at the outcome. It is important to remember that we have an external body that until death we need to keep in top condition so that we may spend as much time as we can on this learning plane we call the earth plane.

Script of 11.3.95 I will not bore the reader with the bulk of this script as it mainly refers to the fact of the aborted career change of my husband that Dad came forward with:-

There is different technology all the time and John will be looked after as this progresses, blend this with our healing and all will be solved quite quickly bringing peace and harmony. "*YES*" *Send us a thought now and again, it keeps us going.* Now blessings go to all the family, especially to your niece Tara with the birth of her baby. We have seen it but we are not allowed to say whether it is a boy or girl only to say that Barbara and Brian will cherish the little mite, a happy occasion as we also feel when the passing of a living form comes to us here with Re-birth. This goes both ways, do you understand? "YES"

Love and best wishes then if we are to close.
Be our little angel of the living and our guiding light.
God Bless from all who are here today with our love and special hugs.
XXXXX

Script of 5.4.95 *Hello Lesley we have been waiting for your contact, my mother asks if she is welcome.* "YES" *Thank you. Dad is here. My little daughter in the portrait, what a likeness! We watched Sarra paint it with such pains and taking great care. Sarra has such a gift and did you know she is back in a spiritual circle again? You will be proud to see her go from strength to strength. She has the ability to tap into the psyche at any given time, so if you both arrange it at the same time you will connect and pass messages to one another. Give it a try when you are abroad and not able to telephone one another, this will expand both of your psyches.*

You are in for a long session with us this evening as there are three generations with us including your Grandma Goodacre making a concentrated effort in contact, we could go on all night, but we won't. We didn't know that your Dad seems quite shocked in hearing that he was the last to know that he had become a great Grandad for the first time. We hear he is to be named Luke, born of Tara and Mick, their first child and first grandchild for Barbara and Brian. Dad says wonderful and the drinks are on him my love, we are gathered to hear this news from you and we thank you and our love is abound. May we bless this great grand child with all the goodness in the workings of every day's life as you know it on your earthly plane. Our mission today is to be worthy of you, our platitudes are a number, because we love you! Cheer up? You'll soon be your old self again! When does Sarra leave for her new job? It's not settled! We will have to look into this she would be silly to move before June as she is owed so much for her love and patience in such awful trying circumstances. May we say our hopes and prayers will hasten an adequate approval in the offing for her? Let us see shall we! She can get her own messages if you help her to do it on her own. Maybe you are lacking in finesse on such a delicate subject with it being your daughter and being that you are too close to the situation in hand. She responds quite negatively at times, so tell her or show her this script: -

Sarra by the end of July your life will have changed completely and a NEW BEGINNING. Before we take our leave however may we share with you that it has been a very pleasant day here today, with lots of loved ones arriving and plenty of family gatherings as our world is united in the fact that whatever and whenever necessary help is needed we are always at hand.

We feel we must go now, with all our love,
THE CLAN XXXXX
G.G. & Dad.(Grandad)

Dear Reader, the above script heralded a newborn into our family, and a warning for Sarra of an ultimate change in her life with a move to Southampton to start a new career, a very big transformation was about to take place. I know she trusted her gut instincts on all of this, plus of course with the help of her own transcripts from spirit, which she confided to me at the time, having shown her my above script.

Also the picture she painted for my birthday was taken from an old hand-painted photograph of myself aged four years standing on a settee between my parents holding a piece of knitting which I used to carry everywhere made up from my first comfort blanket. In the forties it was common practice to paint in the colours on a brown and cream photo, and Dad was right, it is a striking resemblance of all three of us, even capturing dad biting his lip which he did when he was nervous, in his de-mob suit and mum in her forties plaid suit.

CHAPTER 5

INTERCONNECTION WITH SPIRIT AND MORE ASTRAL WAY OF LIFE

Script of Easter Sunday 1995 *Hello darling all our love to you. Were you pleased with your contact today at church then? So you should be it took a lot of us to get through to the medium for your contact as her channel was rather weak. We are more able to convey messages straight to you, hence the cryptic messages given to you, this being the only way to get over what we wanted to say. Our blessings to you and the family and please convey our wishes to Jess and Gwen on this festive occasion. We all wanted our two-penneth at church but were unable to do so; we make amends with the following.*

Firstly we think Sarra has got her sights set, but you still have many unanswered questions! Is this correct? Ok! John will definitely get the job offered, but he is not sure if he is doing the right thing, get reassurance from the medical profession as we are inclined to think that the doctors will play it safe. There is no firm diagnosis yet we do see a different way of life for you but not yet and it may be a little different than you now think of! The firm could make him wait but never the less you'll bring happiness to our little band wherever life sends you! Our blessed ones are always aiming to do the best they can! Be close to the knowledge as we give it to you and nothing will go wrong.

Your health needs a close eye too, so look after yourself and if you are tired then rest, take no notice of what John says he's just being unkind. You're not being lazy; he's just not supporting you. You should know him by now.

Barbara and Brian must be doting grandparents by now, give the little mite our love and so say all of us!!!

My dear sweet child there is nothing you can't do if you put your mind to it! Being of a generous nature and with your love for your fellow human beings who will see you through for as you give so shall you receive and blessed are the pure in heart as the saying goes. Be careful of not rushing around so much though as we want you to be there with us on your Earth plane for some time yet as we have a lot in store for you on the paths of spiritualism. You can bank on us to do your bidding and we would in turn be honoured to do so.

Uncle Joe is fine Lesley, we got your thought/message. He arrived onto our plane yesterday and is convalescing at the moment. The progression of souls to this world is sometimes a severe shock and in Joe's case this was because of the suddenness for him. We knew it was to happen as he was ready for his ascension. We were able to help him come through it relatively simply but he still needed to come to terms with his passing.

Another way of our world is to oversee the living to help with their earthly decisions and if they wish to ignore us then it is their choice making the circumstances far worse than what could have been. Thus we are not allowed to influence some decisions made as we would be blamed and you and others would not be pleased with us. Our knowledge is quite great here concerning certain individuals that we would especially want to help and serve or share our particular faith, so we would not let you take the wrong pathway in life darling so please trust us in this!

Behind all great people there is a guiding light and if that person follows this light to its conclusion many feats are experienced.

Thank you dear, for this has been a good communication but when will you pluck up the courage to do this for others more than you are at present! Start now then Grandad says. We know you are ready my sweet child. We hear what you are saying, that you wish to have more experience with more than this form of clairvoyance! Silly girl you don't need any other form of communication. This is just fine! We are abundantly aware this concept is unusual to take down what is being channelled rather than that of the usual mediums, but it is equal to any other form, after all the dialogue is still the same or even more perfected and the written form is easier to understand.

Further more speech or subliminal messages from spirit are often more tiring for us than coming through the direct link to the brainwaves making the effort to write a much more relaxed and natural way to communicate. This is more natural to us as in the ethereal body we mainly use the thought rather than speech to communicate to each others here for a quick response.

May we take this opportunity to ask how your mother is as we have not received a cry for help for some time! Is our healing sent to her working? Please give us a regular update as your father always asks, especially when he is unable to be present at our link ups, we can always keep him up to date. You can heal yourself you know, and you will find in time, with confidence, it will be a natural process when coming in contact through your medium-ship work which has now begun.

Our world here is quite strict in a different way to yours. It is of oneself. If you do not punish yourself no-one else would, and this self discipline is good for your soul (or spirit). We have larger communities than that of the earth plane and we are very close in harmony with each other with our days and nights quite fulfilling with lots to do for the more inquisitive of us but most settling for contact healing. We all take an occupation here of that which suits one's character. Our pleasure is yours and your plane is ours at times of yours or our choosing.

Because of the loving bond that family ties bring, families usually stick together when ascension takes place as it gives us a greater confidence in whatever we choose to do as we confer together. In this way our elders can give us guidance to pass onto others or just to ourselves. But at the end of the day it is up to that individual to follow up with this given guidance or not!

Well dear we are ready to come to a close and to let you rest; it has been a marathon for you tonight and a sheer delight for us.

Goodnight and God bless from all The Clan.

XXXXXXXXXXXXXXXXXX

E. (Eko - Second Bridging Guide)

Dear Reader, as you can see this extract was indeed a longer one to the norm but I think it gives a marked view on astral life this being the first of many such insights.

Scripts of 23/24 April 1995 *Hello darling, only a few lines today as it is your day and our night. Mary is here with you today. She is your great grandmother and Auntie Margaret Dad's sister who wishes to be remembered. Blessings are coming to you but please change the pen as it seems to be a little blobby. That's started some laughter with those who are here! That's better! We will now continue. We know of your exploits lately and are pleased with your efforts even though you are so critical of yourself when not getting messages across quite right you do give a strong likeness of those who wish to pass on a message. This pathway can continue to be given as long as you run it alongside this one being the written form, enhancing your efforts. Tom, Margaret's husband is here and they both send their love, also John's Uncle Bill in spirit wishes to send Auntie Nell on the earth plane his love.*

Blessings and guidance will always be with you Darling.

Bye for now,

The Clan XXXXXXXX

XXXXX

XXX

X Mum Shepherd.

Script of 23.10.95 *Hi Lesley we are here. We understand there is a dilemma as to whether you have sold your house and we are here to send our thoughts to help the lady in question who was most impressed to go along with the sale, so go and put your deposit on that bungalow you are so taken with. Don't forget we had a hand in the choice too as we know you will be very happy there, also how could she resist your charms at the present moment.*

Dad, Haidee and Uncle Bill all wish you happy birthday for yesterday.

Keep meeting people and we can help them in their endeavours through their own spiritual families to spread our way of life to the ends of the earth in the hope that peace can reign once again.

Our brave child who will now spread her wings for us. The wisdom flows like raindrops from a golden sky, known on high as the emblem of your world. This is being spoken to you from your bridging guide.

Dad says it is a stressful thing when moving. Do not be afraid to take a break from everything, church commitments and your commitment to spirit, so that we can give you a calming and a relaxed state of mind giving strength too, as we know you can't get a quart jug into a pint pot metaphorically speaking. Hard times ahead for a short while because of the impending move with things becoming hectic at times, so take heed of what your family are telling you dear.

"YES Lesley" it is Pancho one of your first gatekeeper guides speaking, did you realize the different vibration of energy that I give off "WELL DONE".

Auntie Ethel here says she is relatively new to the fold but even she realizes the power of communication and to send Uncle Bob her love to her dear husband. Of course she understands if you can't. We have informed her that a message given to a loved one has to be receptive first, and she may have to wait to give it to him in person i.e. on his passing, in reply she asks if he is OK! YES! Thank you!

Dear Reader, I asked Auntie Ethel how she was doing health-wise as she had severe Alzheimer's on passing over and Uncle Bob had found communication with her very difficult. Her reply was that all her normal faculties had returned on entering the spirit realm. This was refreshing to learn as my mother and Bob's sister Gwen is showing early signs of this very debilitating disease. I have been able to assure her in one or two of her more lucid moments that one day she will be able to meet up with the many friends and relations of whom she misses terribly including her parents, two brothers and a sister who have entered spirit world before her.

I recall whilst on the phone on one of her rare lucid moments, mum saying that she wished my father was here as she missed him and then in the next breath she said, never mind I'll see him one day won't I. As I write in 2004 Gwen aged 83 is residing in a nursing home due to her illness. I have been living in Spain for some time and I find it very difficult to engage in conversation with her over the phone as she does not understand who I am and is unable to express how she is feeling, which makes it very hard to come to terms with, and as daft as it sounds to some of you out there, I can't wait for the day of having our special lengthy conversations upon her ascending to the spirit world. All her full faculties will return including the absence of incontinence and frailty that she is enduring at this time along side her basic illness. I comfort myself by having the thought that maybe it is nature's way of preparing me for that fateful day of when I must let her go!

If you find yourself in this position please try and communicate with your loved ones after their passing, this will help the grieving process for both parties. This does not need to go through a third party such as a sensitive, just relax and put pen to paper with a certain conviction that the link WILL be made. With the mind's thought being an extension to the flow of the pen, you don't even have to vet what is written till later, don't forget families stick together in this, and if you ask for their help they will never let you down. I also send my love to you, on your endeavours in making your spiritual connections. I do hope they will be as fruitful as mine have been and always will be.

The above script ended with Dad sending a hug from him whom I feel at times, even as I write and peruse the above script, giving me feelings of sadness.

Also a parting shot within the script from Pancho saying that happiness and sadness are a close link to take this as a strong bond of love rather than sending the usual,

Love from The Clan with the usual kisses,
& Yours Forever Dad X.

Script of 2.11.95 *Hello darling, nice of you to contact us on such a glorious earth day, however you must endeavour to get out and about in it more. Enjoy the peace and beauty that nature can bring to the very soul of one's being thus relieving the stress you know. Go on, give it a try, you need to trim your life down for the pleasures of it more, do you understand? You can't work at the pace you have been doing of late for much longer. You have to be prepared for the upsurge in your working environment and we want to be certain that you have regained enough stamina to cope with it. Insight is worth a lot my darling child, and our abilities to give you strength and endurance will be noticeable!*

Mankind has a lot to offer us at the moment and your insight and the giving of is invaluable to us, we communicate so well because when we are so close to you we feel the need to expand your abilities. Please try! You will be astounded by the success of blending business with pleasure without tiring yourself out.

Well my sweet you feel the need to go about your household chores now. We fully understand, but we thank you for the chat until another time presents itself, we hope soon.

From your ever faithful friend P.
(Pancho - My first Gatekeeper Guide)
xxxxxxx

Script of 10.11.95 *Hello darling child, it has been awhile! Are you sitting comfortably? "GOOD". Well we will begin with our guidance which will become ever increasing as the pressures of your daily life decrease.*

Pancho is speaking through us today and she says that she was so pleased with your communication with her and her Comanche family being so successful through your friend Elaine. This may or may not make sense to you but the closer you come to our realm the plainer things become in your world, our love is so strong to those we love and adore, when things are not always what they seem you must experiment a little. Incidentally we know you are blessed with a good nature but there are some people that could exploit this, so do be careful not to be drawn into anything against your will or what may not feel right, and our plans for you are so exciting you will not want for anything in your twilight years.

We urge you to get rid of the too large a property, for now is the time to let go of some of the trappings of life. May we also add that on this sphere of life we do not have this problem we just materialize what kind of abode, if any that we wish to reside in, so we are lucky in this respect.

However because you have such a difference, we do understand such pressures placed upon you and your kind have in your world, and with a little faith we can help to alleviate some of them, so do lean on us. That is what family is all about "ALIVE OR DEAD".

Dad is here now and says he always gets left out now that you have your own guide. Do you think he is jealous? He say's, my darling you are my only existence on the earth plane that I can speak with, so please don't forget to keep contact with me on this side.

We now hand you over to Pancho. I believe that you had a sitting with one of your parishioners and that Elaine showed the likeness of me (Pancho) within her trance-like state and also that of my brother and grandfather. Were you able to understand the snippets I gave to you about my tribe and my existence on the earth plane many years ago? This gift of showing a likeness of spirit over shadowing you (transfiguration) will also come your way in time as you grow with your medium-ship. Bringing Love and Laughter with those who truly believe in the guiding light of spirit, and lives changing immeasurably because of it as we know how to become your friend for the goodness of others, do let yourself become a leader so we can start to teach your world to be a better place to exist in.

We understand you are to rest more so with your permission we take our leave and we pass you over to your healing guide who wishes to be of assistance to you as we now say goodbye.

From your ever loving,
Clan & P.
xxxxx

Dear Reader, the above script referred to a lady called Elaine whom I befriended at my local spiritual church who could also do spiritual writings as her medium-ship, along with a natural gift of healing and I felt we both had an affinity of parallel pathways sharing a fascination on the subjects of the Egyptian and Lemurian way of life. She had also talked of a close encounter of a sighting of an unidentified flying object which hovered some feet away from her whilst standing at a bus stop and then in an instant it was gone. This parallel also prompted me to share with her some of my E.T. scripts coming through to me in 1997 to the present day of 2008 as I write.

With very little prompting we decided to do a joint sitting at my home where she went into a trance like state with a blending and sharing a vibration of energy I was then able to experience my first occasion of seeing my spirit guide overlaying Elaine's body. She had her head turned towards the wall but my guide's likeness was looking straight at me. Her hair at this time was a flowing mane of long black straight hair and with each manifestation, of which she showed me three, the first was Pancho, and I was able to sketch her later as a braided squaw with large blue eyes. After a chat with her another manifestation of her brother, an Indian brave, also braided and portraying similar features was then followed by an elderly looking chief with the same beguiling blue eyes, but with very grey long lank hair with the son's braided headdress which included a prominent feather upwards and another drooping down at the side attached to the braided headband.

I might add that Elaine had really dark brown eyes and the hair difference was very pronounced. The grandfather of Pancho started to speak through Elaine telling me that his son's name was Broken Arrow which made sense to me due to the attire. He had also told me that he and Pancho had been with me since birth and were helping me with my development including my healing of others. I should be aware of the many changes of my body manifesting themselves as my guiding forces will change as my commitments change. He gave me many instances of the Comanche way of life, but most of all this occasion impressed on me that with every startling change of apparition, I distinctly remember quietly saying to Elaine that I wished that she could see what I was seeing. I might add all this appeared to be like an old black and white image as if from an ancient projector such as used in Charlie Chaplin's day which was flickering over her face as I focused on Elaine's images. When she needed to pull away and my vibration concentration of energy drained, Elaine appeared quite normal once again. That moment will stay with me forever.

I am sorry to report that when I bumped into her recently she had felt that under someone else's influence she needed to destroy all her scripts, and to my knowledge she has turned her back on the spirit world using her prerogative to tread her own pathway forward as she deemed fit. This proves to me that if you wish to be master of your own destiny, spirit will oblige at any time and stand aside.

But will you be as happy? And what a sad loss!

I still feel, even a decade later, very excited and privileged to be part of such a close bond.

Script of 30.11.95 *Hello Darling, what a surprise. We are over the moon for the contact, we have been trying to impress on you to pick up the pen to go over what you have been experiencing of late. Our powers are getting stronger and your senses are sharpening, have you felt this? It is a natural progression here. We have flashes all the time on our sphere; it is natural to see images in a sepia way as well as colour. We are not always sure what is happening, we just know how we see!*

Your thoughts are correct, because we have a little insight we are able to tell you your leading pathway. For instance, our premonition for you is that we see a cottage like a bungalow on a hill overlooking green pastures as far as the eye can see. Wonderful for your artistic capabilities! Yes, you can, or will be able to afford this abode, no problem, and we know you will be happy there as we have already blessed this home for you. You will both be more settled with this move and the cheaper lifestyle will enable you to go abroad once more for your holidays, and as you both mix amongst the peoples, God's work will be done three fold. Our wavelength with you now shortens dear so we must take our leave of you.

From your guiding spirit for now xxxxxx

Dear Reader, a new signature of a double 8 super-imposed denoted a new guide had been in charge, also giving me a different feel of energy through and around me ready for 1996 to be heralded in. A VERY GOOD SIGN.

Script of 1.12.95 *Hello Lesley. Well darling you are a wonderful mother but you can't burden yourself with your children's responsibility, they must do this for themselves. You can only guide them and be there for them as the inevitable situations arise, and as you mean a lot to them they will hold back. You also need your strength for your impending move.*

We love you and your family on the earth plane and will not let any of them come to unnecessary harm, but sometimes life throws up many lessons to learn on a personal level, do you not agree?

United blessings my child as we leave you, and please confide in us any time if you think we can allay your fears.

GOD BLESS XXXXXX
From The Clan.

Dear Reader, this indeed was spirit's way of trying to tell me of an impending split for my daughter, which proved to be a painful affair all around. I had no power over my daughter as she has my strong will and an instinctive spiritual guidance of her own when things are not working out and also how to put things right in any given situation, such as moving many miles away to heal the rift, and in doing so finding a stronger love in her life. She sealed this love with the bearing of two wonderful children in the same year also giving my husband and I great pleasure.

This script taught me that this was another chapter in my life's rich tapestry, where we as parents can take it upon ourselves to try and heal our children's hurt, even though they are quite capable of seeing it through by themselves and we have to have the courage to stand back a little.

Script of 2.12.95 *Hello Darling we are so sorry that the heartache is still with you from yesterday. A mother's lot is not always a happy one. On our plane you choose your partner for his quality of mercy, it would not be right if given days were to come and go without any challenges in life. On this sphere of life we welcome them, even those challenges of help given on the earth plane we have to first discuss as a family on this side of life, before intervening on any issues raised for the good of those individuals we still call family on the earthly plane, and as such, the spirit people here flock to see what will be next on our saga. It's better than any of your soaps. No, your are not quite Ena Sharples, or Elsie Tanner. Someone here says 'Err' Hilda Ogden! 'No', we are only jesting. Sorry we are digressing.*

Our nuptials are different from that of yours on the earth plane as we get pleasure from the fact that we have given pleasure, and only then do we get our satisfaction of a good days work done. We endeavour to give our best shot and have the power to guide the right path individually but not together if necessary with some couples. After all we didn't do a bad job on you two with a little help and guidance, be truthful now. You both belong together even though you have been sorely tested many times in your 37th year of marriage as you are typing this. Look how strong you both are now! With both of you getting the up-most out of life individually making the partnership stronger.

Wait and see my sweet child, given from your bridging guide

and also love from The Clan,
Especially in your hour of need. God Bless. Xxxx

Dear Reader, the above script proved that the break up would go ahead and that the future was not quite as bleak as it was first imagined and that we had brought our child up to be a person in her own right whether we liked it or not, and that we as parents had to go along with whatever decision she made. The priority was her happiness. How many of you can relate to this dilemma? Quite a few I suspect.

Incidentally, the double 8 signature popped up again on the sign off, thus logging off as a bridging guide from another world's spiritual existence. I know there will be many more guiding links of this nature to come to me in the years ahead. I look forward to this phase of existence as an exciting one for me, and excited with what I may offer to you and many of my readers to come.

Script of 11.12.95 *Hello darling so pleased to hear from you, as things improve on the home front we are saying to you today that Sarra has two paths open to her and the choice is hers to take without hurting herself and others, for if she leaves it too long it will be harder for her, so we are urging her to move now! You can guide her, but we will choose the time and the written word to help her, so please take our blessings on your endeavours and be guided by us. We will not fail, we promise! Looking to the future is a different thing. We will guide her beyond all measure of experience as once we have given a promise there is no going back. This goes both ways so be careful of what you both wish for as you both have the ability to make things work against all odds.*

Stronger and stronger, as days go by, your very special gift of learning is growing within. We can feel this, do you? We amply reward those who help to give us eternal life and we are so pleased you have chosen to join our elite band of followers, with the full knowledge that you will guide strangers who may stray onto your pathway, as love and truth always show their true feelings.

A spiritual mother is a very special mother indeed as Sarra loves and trusts you to show her the light,

with God's Speed.
From all of us here. The Clan & your spiritual Guides.

Dear Reader, I was indeed truly blessed with the above script as there were six signatures at the close of it, showing me that I was not alone with my family problems and that I could share anything with them and get peace of mind as I trust them, this being not just my arisen members of my family but also from the ministering angels that are around us at all times.

1996

Script of 4.1.96 *Hello darling welcome to a new year heralding in with it many changes. "YES" we are all here to wish you a very happy new year and do we have a surprise for you my darling child, we had assembled just in case, it is such a pleasure to welcome you.*

Our many friends on this side are pulling out all the stops for you and yours, hoping to make changes for the better, and from your bridging guides who have a high regard for your planet, they are saying that your world is forever changing, but more so this year. As you become closer to our way of life you will find you are given higher blessings that are easily accepted, so at this present time, on your spiritual front our family blessings echo with theirs.

However you must be patient a little longer as strings are being pulled on your behalf to quicken your sixth sense. We have news that a pleasant surprise is on the way for you and not before long, for as we speak there is much discussion as to what is best for you and the most highest of us claim that we must make that decision for you.

Grandad and your father are here to say that they have always known, even as a child, you have been wiser than your years, and we know of you to play things close to your chest for a while as certain successes come about, but do remember us when you rejoice in these as we are to be pre-informed with them along with any failures.

Well we must close now with many blessings from all of us and especially Grandad who says you are his favourite and not to forget him especially now that your Father has ascended to be here with us on this side of life. Dad says that Mum will be pleased to see how well the both of us get on over here through the many communications we have built up over the years and we are sure she will be very happy in our little throng of activity, also we will introduce her to those who have stayed in our fold just to welcome any newcomers dropping in too on many occasions.

Goodbye and God Bless from your Family.

Script of 12.1.96 *Hello Darling we are here just waiting to speak to you, once again how time flies. May we say things are improving, and by the way your strange visitor last night was indeed one of us, we would like to say a health visitor. "NO" not a member of your family but one of our healers, did you see him? "WELL" Congratulations we must give you more spiritual sight then.*

We know you are at the start of your giftedness and we can help in this area which in turn will help when giving communication with your earthly bound insight when helping others. Our difficulties have been as to know how much or how little vibration of energy to give you. Your health has to be monitored each time when giving you a boost to help with either relieving stress or to just boost the level of contact vibration.

So may we take a perfect day and make it better YES

May we say things to console you YES

May we honestly put things to rights YES

We could go on for ever YES

We need to say we are sorry, we are here to help

and the tears flowing with our little quote to you means when you are close to us in this way we are able to dispel any negative emotional needs as a cleansing takes place.

Darling please may we ask you to endeavour to try and keep this form of communication flowing back and forth to us, as we do it so well. PROMISE! Good girl say all of us.

While we speak of Astral insight may we also say that those who think of the animal kingdom when they pass, automatically linking into spirit as you do when a friend loses their pet or you see a fallen animal by the side of your roads, with that thought we uplift their souls in much the same way as ordinary mortals and we make sure that that animals' Etheric body gets taken to their own mortal porthole here to be reunited with their own kind while they wait to be with their masters or mistresses if need be.

Dad says he loves you and will help to protect you and Sarra's Grandma (Haidee) is saying she will help to watch over her from spirit too. We say that she is redeeming herself with this effort and we think that she will do a good job, so please send her the message above for us. Thank you.

As for yourself your probationary period is over, get out there and help others. Dad also wants to send his love to Sarra. Our guide here tells us you had a try at healing with mum and we could see it bringing an improvement to her body when you had gone due to your abilities, thus showing that it was a strong force of healing, vibration wise that is, which only enforces the need to transfer the same to others whilst in contact with them through us, in much the same way that you did today. Be guided by us and you'll not go far wrong.

Well we must go for now, with our love forever, and a special one from Dad to say thanks for helping Mum.

The Clan xxxxxxx

Dear Reader, my father's thanks on the above script appertains to a visit to my mother's house. She sat on the settee looking quite frail chattering away with myself seated on Dad's favourite armchair. I saw her face and body glowing as she chattered on and I felt a sudden physical discharge of energy flowing between us, so much so it took a little while before I felt able to answer her. I found that with the script above mentioning that it is quite natural to give healing to a loved one in this way especially when you realise you are just passing on a divine source. So do try this for yourselves. It is so easy and you could help your elderly parents in the same way. I view this as a pure and solid link to do good, especially when all other avenues of medical help has been sought. It is a pure energy of love that seems to be the key to wanting to make the recipient better.

As I leave this chapter you have probably realised that I was becoming more used to my thought process changing where spiritual conceptions were concerned. So now I lead you onto my next turning point focused within the next chapter.

Tara's wedding.

This portrait will appear on the front cover of the third book *A Diary through Spirit Masters to Masters.*

My first Gatekeeper Bridging guide Munchien. The Spiritual Artist was impressed to draw my guides in the way that she has, giving me her medium's advice that this Guide was to be connected to me in Spain where I now reside some two years after the sitting with her.

CHAPTER 6

SPIRITUAL CONCEPTIONS INCLUDING TUTORING ETC.

Script of 4.2.96 *Hello Darling surprise, surprise you made it! We have been trying to impress upon you to sit with the pen and get in touch with us as we would like to give more on the home front for you. Your move is still going ahead and there are a lot of changes for the better on the way. Clearly you are a woman in your own right and not hiding in John's shadow for the first time within this lifetime, and only good can come of it as you strive forward doing things for yourself. You are presenting a guiding light for others to follow.*

So far we have here your Dad, Mum H, Auntie Ada and Uncle Bill from the Clan of your spiritual family and our own leader with many other newcomers to this world as we are now a teaching platform for others to follow in this path towards enlightenment.

To succeed on this plane of life in our spirit realms we must prove our worth and you have been a worthy alliance in this. Your blessings have been small but very significant, especially the snippets you are showing us of life's eternal struggles, and how the changes of generation after generation have to cope with a demanding world to which you and all mankind have to deal with.

We are all well aware that we have to be responsible in the manner to which we convey knowledge to you and what you actually give out physically speaking.

We all hope that we can make a difference to the love and positivity that can be passed to one another rather than the negativity that quite often takes place.

Our only vice being that we take up most of your valuable time but also it is worth mentioning that on this plane our being here is to learn from our past lives' mistakes and to carry forward on a better pathway this time around taking with us any teachings which may be given to be shared.

You are now to take an easier pattern of life for the next six months for we need you to take the next evolution at a much higher level to be of use to us when you return to this plane. In our keeping you will become a very high entity, energy-wise that is.

We know your path has not been easy so far with a lot of opposition from your earthly members which sorely tested you but it has been worth it from our point of view as we had to find out if you were worthy to carry on year after year as you have done. Believe us when we say that you will not want for anything as we always reward those who have such love in their hearts for their fellow man. By showing no judgement when another comes to seek advice and the connection of giving healing for the soul's energy and Etheric body which enhances the physical body to help self- healing in many instances.

My sweet child there is much fascination in your world as to how transgression takes place, meaning from your plane to ours. We need more souls of your calibre to keep a momentum going to help mankind learn from one another that the existence of life after death does exist.

In fact our truer existence happens to be here and

not there on your plane. On your earthly plane one would learn the pitfalls of life but on our plane it is a more substantial element of learning to tutor onwards. You will find that your knowledge will grow stronger with more contact and your energy level will grow to keep up with this. We alone will be the ones who know how far to push you at this present time given the pathway you have chosen this time around before you ascend once more.

A word of warning here - your gift is our gift to you and as such can be taken away at any time. This has been proven many times with other mediums who became famous then suddenly, because of their greed, because of not receiving any messages started to make things up or to elaborate on them, this is so dangerous as the sense of behaving responsibly towards others becomes misleading with many dire consequences.

From your family here Dad wishes to send his love to you and not to forget him, as if you would. He is also conveying that he is trying to impress upon your mum that she will be joining him, along with many of her long arisen friends here quite soon. Your days with her are limited although this is not yet imminent as she has some living yet to do.

With your existing knowledge of this way of life you will be able to cushion her way of thinking and let go of her earthly shell gracefully. Upon the arisen state she will find a new life exists with a fulfilling body and state of mind. We will help her when her time comes.

We know this will be hard for you but we will be there with you every step of the way impressing on you what to say at what ever given time as it presents itself to you.

May we say goodnight for now my darling daughter before you run out of paper.

From all The Clan.
WE LOVE YOU xxxxx
and from your guiding light here.
GOD BLESS x

Script of 12.2.96 *Hello Darling nice to hear from you. Well, well, aren't we the clever one then, your first multi-sitting! The force was quite strong with you and we are pleased you are now putting into practice that which we have been instilling in you for some time. We are so proud of your success after such a short while. If you keep going people are going to be most impressed with you too. We all had a great time listening in and partied afterwards as it has been a long time coming, so now believe us and stop dabbling and try in earnest. May we also say that you chose the right girls (one of these being Elaine whom I have previously spoken of and she gave very factual messages which helped all those present) to hold your first home circle and one of us here says that is how it should be if you want to grow strongly with spirit communication. We also joined in the laughter as we are not offended, we do not expect it to be serious all the time. You did just fine let's hope this is just the beginning.*

My darling child we are backing you 100% from now on to go about your business in a more proficient manner starting a new career and we will make it easy for you to survive so that you may give us some of your time once in awhile. My dear sweet child we know you have misapprehensions about this but everyone has to start somewhere and this is definitely it!!!

Let us stay together in this, after all without you we cannot shine with our abilities so we send our blessings in abundance to renew your efforts. It is a step further forward on the earth peace trail as we would like to look at it in this way. After all mankind can learn so much with yours and our help to blossom and grow with all our little seeds in mind and body enriching them to go from strength to strength, this is given to you from the higher minds.

So go with it your way getting stronger with time as no one person can tell you how and where to begin. We only want what is best for you and will never let any harm befall you.

There is only a short time left this evening so we must part. Get in touch with us again, but before we go one more point to say and that is we ALL love you very much and you have been the chosen one from the start of this life this lifetime around so build up the power as much as you can while you are there, and oh what a surprise you'll have when you arrive here.

Love and best wishes from THE CLAN X
And your present guides in the spirit world.

Dear Reader, as you may have come to the conclusion by now from the above scripts which helped me so much at the time, be reassured that if given similar information as this, your progression forward will take place.

When with caution you tap into the inspired side of your nature and bring forward your inquisitiveness towards spiritual connections always date the information before you start your inspired work and get whatever entities to sign off. With the best will in the world you could not memorise every signature and style of writing you will be given, and whereby you may have thought it had come from your natural sense the material in actual fact has been given to you from a spiritual sixth sense perspective.

Script of 23.2.96 *Hello again to you my dear sweet child your guide here, may I say you are well blessed with protection at the moment and never again will any ill befall you. (This means a protected aura of light to stop any other spiritual connections.) At present the guidance you are receiving is very impressive indeed as there is much to do in this lifetime span, THE PLAN is much in evidence.*

Starting within the new millennium period you are to go abroad to live and use this knowledge for it will become a magical place especially with your beliefs. Even your sister Barbara will encourage this move though at present she is concerned with her health and needs you to use your new found ability of healing, so use it and you will find more and more people flocking to you once this newfound ability strengthens and this particular gift of yours grows. Also many will be taught by you to do the same, more so in the new country where you will eventually reside. God Bless your efforts on this new vocation, never have we known such a willing pupil.

Can we also add whilst on this subject, that you may not realize the changes that are being made in your psychic field! We do know that with the connections to your church, whilst they have helped you to come to terms with these changes you have outgrown their protocol. They have helped to retain a sense of responsibility when dealing with the public over the many years but there is a need to move onto pastures new now. The need to help your fellow man has increased as you feel the higher vibrations flowing throughout your body.

We are aware you had a dream recently of a cottage with red roses around the door and you having a red shawl around your shoulders. Significantly this dream was induced by your grandmother; she is saying that she put the red flannel cloth around your shoulders to enhance the energy and healing that your ethereal body needed at that moment. She has been chosen to oversee your medical needs at this present time of stress. Dad says not to forget his input in this area too.

May we say you have a very loving and caring family on this plane and your earthly one too. It is refreshing in the fact that you have accepted our existence here so readily along with most of mankind that you meet. You endeavour to instil an inner peace which comes flowing through with the knowledge given in abundance to you at times as you reach a higher frequency of thought whilst linking into us.

We will say again we will never let you down. Keep us on our toes by keeping the inquiring mind open with lots of questions for us to answer.

Your John seems to be more cautious than you are but rest assured the move will take place when you are both happy with the situation, so just let it happen in its own time darling. All we wish for you and your family on the earth plane is a happy home life and a rosy future. Sarra's split is inevitable as she has a strong sixth sense just like her mother, but just like you she will find another to match her own.

When your mother ascends to come home here again, the pain you felt on your father's passing will not be so devastating for you as he promises to be there to help both with her transition and to boost your feelings, thus taking the burden of such grief sharing with the up-liftment afterwards making a stronger bonding from this world to yours.

Be assured that families stay together both on the learning ground we call earthbound and here on this plane once re-united. Here on this plane of life is such a wonderful setting.

It is one that you cannot start to imagine.

Each individual chooses his or her lifetime span before beginning their rebirth on the earthly plane. Lessons have to be learnt on the earth bound plane first. Each individual spirit is given permission to move onto a higher plane of existence upon arriving here rather than returning for another progressive life to relearn but in a different way. This progressive learning process or what we call freedom of spiritual movement is assessed by each individual's masters (Guides) and evaluated by their peers in this world called the hierarchy (the Angel realm). To put it simply "it's like living in a goldfish bowl down here on earth" a mortal link once said to us.

As time runs out with us yet again we send our total love and gratitude with the pathway you have chosen to tread. We ask you to build the power up as much as you are able and what a surprise you will have here upon returning to your spiritual home once again, especially with the benefits you will have gained.

Love and Best wishes from the highest realm of Tutor and two loving members of your family

Dad and Grandma xxxxxx

Dear Reader This guidance given is very evident at all times. Pushing one's very soul and the mind's expansion onwards to higher happenings every single day, that is, if you are brave enough to let it happen on a regular basis. Also the premonitions given there were two moves. One to a bungalow in Hinckley with lots of rose bushes and I am writing this in the 2000's hoping that you will all get to read the finished article spurred on by my guides to write not one, but many books with the ongoing material still flowing through me by the pen.

Script of 1.3.96 *Hello darling, blessings are to you and your family and ours. Your guide here says excellent work last night; our little bird has taken flight. In regards to the knowledge that you gave as we relayed to you when helping one of the brethren at church, there is to be another good deed to do for us again my sweet, as other families ask if messages and connections through you can be sought. We predict that John has only a few years with his company and taking early retirement with a good pay settlement and then your first move. Time to take sustenance, we are indeed lucky as we have no need to fortify a solid body such as yours, our energy field is enough for us to survive, clever eh!*

Stop worrying over things that are out of your control and spend more time on your gardening says Dad, you know how he loved it so, this will focus the mind once again and give you so much pleasure, seeing the bulbs poking through of snowdrops of pure white, daffodils of bright yellow uplifting the inner spirit, tulips of bright red and crimson giving energy and crocus of the lavender hue for insight, these being the essence of the colours that we live by. Of course in our realm our flowers are everlasting and can be set any time of the year as time is not relevant here.

Now is the time to put your affairs in order, personal and otherwise as great changes of your lifestyle becomes known. A holiday is seen in Ireland for you and some members of your earthly family going with you, and many magical memories too in a lovely cottage rented from a colleague of John's.

Our guidance will be most apparent over the next few days with motivation in abundance, let us say there will be no looking back as we take the reins guiding your life forward at speed, let us prove our worth for once and trust us implicitly. The Clan made up of family connections grows daily in love for you and your kindness, even including children who need comfort when they pass with their closest and dearest, welcoming their spirit form to this world of ours until they are re-united with their parents or grandparents here. As you meet with any of your fellow man please remind them of this fact. We have grown our little group here, like any company you would find earthbound and we endeavour to THRIVE AND SURVIVE, a very good motto to pass on, we never aim to interfere.

Your survival upon ascending will be matched by what you have learnt and the love you hold in your heart. On this note may we wish you happiness in all your endeavours and remember we will be by your side, whether in joy or sadness, to help to uplift you when you are down and soar with the extra energy given off when things go right. Your energy enables us to visit higher realms where we may stay to explore more of what that particular realm has to offer or return to a lower realm not so much out of our comfort zone, much as you mortals decide whether to strive out onto new territory.

Beloved we must take our leave so we hope you have had some enlightenment and do use this form of communication to your guiding lights here at any time when your sixth sense is in need.

Our Love and guidance as always The Clan xxxx

and a special hug from Evelyn. X

P.S. we send Rose Petals to you.

Dear Reader, this piece of text reminded me of a wonderful holiday spent with my sister and her husband along with John my husband in Ireland quite some time after receiving it with many happy memories. These are just a mention of a few. My sister Barbara and I having left our other halves in the pub decided to leave them there and go and prepare dinner. The heavens opened up as we started to stroll then run down the hill to the cottage. Barbara suddenly stopped in the middle of the road and laughing said ‘why are we running’, we are as wet as we are ever going to be. Grinning I turned to her and agreed. A memory we both remind ourselves of now and again to this day, bringing a point to mind that as one goes along this rich tapestry of life there comes a point when we have to make a decision of enough’s enough and stop and take stock.

On another occasion the following year we had taken John’s brother Colin, and Marie his partner to the same place at the same time of year, but this time a wonderful sunny holiday. I recall one afternoon while Marie and Colin were sunbathing in the garden (and I might add Colin came in with a perfect white arm print from Marie on his back, to which we had a giggle over for a few days), anyway I digress. It was a quiet afternoon and I decided to take a book to read in the older part of the cottage where I felt a presence in front of me. On looking up there appeared a spirit form of a lady with Quaker looking clothes on. She looked at me, nodded then disappeared. Unusually I didn’t feel apprehensive, on the contrary I was in her home after all, and she seemed quite pleasant, but that view changed drastically when that night on retiring a most oppressive presence awoke me announcing he was the master and husband of the spirit that had appeared that afternoon. He clearly didn’t like me being there. So in my mind I asked him to leave but he refused. I instinctively recited the Lords Prayer and he vanished with much relief on my part leaving a feeling of calm surge within me. I felt, wow! What the power of instinctive thought has and how quick the angel realm responds.

These Insights of the way that the spirit realms think and their offerings of the good things to look forward to amazes me even to this day in the 2000's when just as I think that I have learnt enough up comes yet another text of fascination.

But please be warned if you try this form of communication for yourself don't forget to protect yourself each time you pick up the pen to write, by asking the angel realm to look after you and your personal guides i.e. a family member you trust or your Gatekeeper if you know him or her of which you have been born with who will make it so.

Then enjoy every magical moment of connection.

Before I leave this script the premonition given did come to fruition with less trepidation than at first expected. Indeed my husband and I are living quite comfortably in retirement and still together after 43 years in the year of 2009. Thanks to the message to put our affairs in order we have been able to plan our twilight years yet to come. I don't feel any older than the inner body which is boosted now and again by my personal healing guide, making me feel 30 plus inside even though in my 60's, but my body lets me down occasionally with the usual stress and strain of life taking it's toll.

I feel privileged to have that special healing connection from such a high source spurring me on to where this unique pathway of success 'as time goes by' is getting better and better, with much delight at times. This I endeavour to pass on to you to maybe help in some way with whatever you may wish to enfold for your future.

Script 16.3.96 *Hi Lesley many thanks in your co-operation in returning to us for a special message from your peers here on a higher plane of life. Firstly we send blessings to your brethren there and afar.*

Look into your hearts at this moment and dwell in the peace of the moment of contemplation. We speak of the evening in Denis and Peter's circle that you and your friend Dora found yourselves joining for further knowledge and to experience the physical phenomena of spirit whereby the channelling of a medium allows spirit to use the physical voice-box to speak through.

You were both chosen well to learn, but under the right conditions, to practice for yourselves. You asked if you were doing right and we can say that we acknowledge both of you as being the right applicants from now on, with a forward motion putting into place to encompass lessons learnt and the trust in us to keep you safe, with an expansion of the network beginning in earnest with only the highest and the best connecting to you. True guidance will be given to you at times with experience coming through the planning and execution of the facts given.

There is a need to link into the minds of our many teachers here only too willing to help to further your knowledge but an extra field of activity in the brain means a deeper meditation to reach them. Never forget this doesn't mean your family will not be there for you as they also need quality time now and again, and they will instinctively connect at the right given moment. After all, you have spent many years building this wonderful bond with your spiritual family, 'known here as your clan', to let them go at a time of a new needed form of channelling.

This will enable you to become more adept when bonding with your own bridging guides from another galaxy.

We leave you now with:-

LAUGH AND THE WORLD LAUGHS WITH YOU!!!

But always remember by being serious occasionally you will find others will take your messages more plausibly, so strike a happy balance when giving survival messages.

Your Peers of this realm wish you farewell for the moment and please contact us again soon on this link of a higher vibration.

Four new signatures followed this script.

Dear Reader At this juncture I have a written format of the meetings at Peter's house where Denis took the notes of the spoken words given by spirit. The material was very interesting as some came from an intergalactic source and I think that it is more applicable to save this for the next book of enlightenment, along with the links I am making at present from 1998 into the 2000's. If you are reading this material you can be rest assured that indeed book number two will be in the publisher's hands shortly, so look out for this – ***A Diary through Spirit Intellectually***.

Script 18.3.96 *Hello darling we are here to welcome you to our world and our leader today says there is no finer recognition than yours. How can we help you? We hear that you have been having some health problems while your ethereal body is being attuned to a higher vibration of energy. This is quite normal as you approach a different outlook on life there will be however from this link a marked improvement so take heart with this knowledge as you feel a betterment of the physical body as well as the inner one, as a strong ethereal body enhances that of the physical. Let things take its natural course then dear and believe in what we are telling you.*

Your spiritual family are here other than Dad who is out visiting loved ones at the moment. He'll be gutted to know he has missed your contact but life goes on, even here. John's Uncle Bill and your Auntie Ethel are here, also Evelyn is asking how Jess your father in-law is coping. She understands that her little Yorkshire terrier Bobby is being taken care of by him and he is helping to comfort him for his loss of her. She says thank him for her. Also may she ask if you can hold him and channel the love through so that she can be reunited temporally by the vibrational link to her beloved pet? We feel this discharge of emotion quite clearly as if we are there on the material plane, and we wish more mortals would give off this energy to help those on this dimension as we are only a few feet away from the mortal realm, it's just that the majority of the mortal realm have yet to learn this.

Our guide here seems to think we have outstayed our welcome but as we take our leave of you we understand you have had a few disturbed nights when the Dunblane disaster took place. Well my dear, you have been doing some soul-retrieval within astral travelling! This is where the inner spiritual body, tethered to the physical body, by the gold or silver Etheric umbilical cord, which is found at the centre of the body, takes flight whilst you are asleep to link up with those leaving the mortal coil suddenly to help guide them home to loved ones here on this spiritual plane. So it is no- wonder you feel tired! Now take it easy for a few days and you will soon be back to your normal self once more.

Time to go now, with love to all and,

Bless You.

Dear Reader, you will find out as you progress through this book, there are quite often times when you should take a note of any bodily changes taking place. Do not be afraid to ask for help with your guides, rather than family in spirit, even if at first you are not fully aware of who they are but still wish to understand the reason for those changes to help your progress forward.

I also learnt that the many disturbed nights I was experiencing at the time were not in vain and therefore putting into context my new learning curve. Feeling aware of a new change taking place for me where my spiritual commitment lay other than the earth plane, and having read the above script I felt quite proud of my achievements thus far with a new found self worth.

Script of 30.3.96 *Welcome darling, the answer is "Yes" to whether you are to accept the secretarial post at church. We will help your spiritual thinking process; do not fear it as you will become King Pin in a short space of time for a long span in Office. Edna will show you the ropes when she realizes that she is in need of a much needed rest. She has been too stubborn to have stepped down before and the change over of a new committee where Diane your friend takes over the reins from Steven giving her the excuse to move down to the lower ranks of the committee. We know you were somewhat bamboozled into the position by Diane your new president. She was quick to see your potential as a colleague as well as a close friend, which over the past year you both have become. Though you are older than her she still thinks you are a youngster where spiritual communication is concerned. We say that she is in for quite a shock as we know how quickly you have developed into a far worthier contender than she believes you to be, but in the end she will come to terms with what you have to offer both for the church and mankind to boot.*

Your destiny is now beginning to take shape as far as we are concerned. There is much learning to be had from both sides you know, so don't run before you are able to walk.

The love you have of people in general will certainly be returned.

God Bless!

Please believe us when we say we have mapped out this part of your life meticulously.

Blessings my dear daughter, Yes! It's your father speaking to you, so do as you're told there's a dear. 'May we collectively say here, here to that?'

Your meeting at church seemed to be conducted a little unfairly but will be seen to be fair as time progresses.

Good luck to you and Diane as this is the finest hour for both of you. Whenever guidance is needed you can rely on us and especially your present guide whose influence of straight speaking out of a purposeful dilemma will be ever present. You will be surprised at the speed of growth that you will make within Stansted's national spiritual movement and will indeed be the envy of most. We are not surprised though, after all let us reflect for awhile why this all began and why it has taken shape in this way. Our knowledge is that your blessed childhood and trials and tribulations were given to you so that in turn you have a lot to give to others, where their unfortunate situations were similar to your own, making you an excellent candidate to console and give advice.

Now let us march onto the intrigue of your abode which we predict will obviously be changed for the better and will be easier to manage and with it you will be blessed with an almost calm atmosphere.

The God Force is with you despite what twaddle was said in the meeting such as the fight within the spiritual movement to remove The Lords Prayer and the removal of your church's large bequeathed bible on the rostrum. Your eloquent speech of having the elderly within your brethren so it should stay we thought was grand, as we believe that the Laws of Eternity is never to be divided in action for the common good. Our teaching is so very different to that. You will ponder over this at present but in time it will become clear!

Go with what you deem fit at the time, we are so proud of you darling. We have a saying here to never let sentiment rule your head and to go with free thought. Explain amongst your peers in the movement and things will flow more smoothly. Try not to let frustration creep in and be on your guard against others that may wish ill of you.

May we also say that Mrs. Dorothy Hudson, the head of the West Midlands District Council, will help you. Though she appears to be a little stern for others to approach her, you will not have a problem as she will take you under her wing as a prodigy. Do you understand dear?

Time to sign off now so God Bless once again,
from those present here and Your New Guide.
XXXXXX

Dear Reader The above script meant so much to me as I was out of my comfort zone with both the close liaison with the National Spiritualist Union, who regulates all their working churches throughout Britain, and the role of secretary to the Hinckley church, and sometimes at odds when trying to do my up-most for those who attended it. I found that within the many years which I gave voluntarily to the church Dorothy Hudson, who at that time was one of the leading members of the unions' West Midlands District Council, to be my closest ally and a role model of how to conduct myself in public. This proved to be a total turn around in my life where I was not just the little wife at home but putting my mark on this world of ours in a profound and constructive way.

Script of 31.3.96 Hello darling, may we say thank you for all your goodness to others, this improvement is always to be the true ongoing you! May we say there are lots more kind thoughts coming your way. As we speak our leaders here are saying that they have not met anyone quite like you for some time. Mankind needs more like you and this is not to be treated lightly. Spread your kind of energy wherever possible and we will indeed see a different planet. You do not wish to be a speaker on the rostrum yet as you feel this would be a little overbearing. We however understand that this quality is indeed in its infant stage and quite possibly we will have to wait for the time when you strive out on your own, maybe abroad instead of the U.K. If so, so be it. We have plenty of time to wait for your glory, to which we will bask in, though we must stress you are ready now! OK! We understand that you are happy to be a chairperson only at your church alongside the many mediums who visit the church. We feel that this would re-unite you both as a couple when John understands your calling and he will become more involved. You wait and see. This we prophesise.

A message now from your dad who is always present, he says one day you will see him again physically speaking. He says it's just as hard for him not to be able to physically cuddle his eldest child too. We are able to say that it is natural for us to be apart from our loved ones once we have acclimatised here on this plane. He of course is one of the lucky ones as you are regularly in touch with him and his so called clan being your family links. There are many who have no such direct link and feel the burden more acutely. Pancho was with you when you stood for the first time at church on the Rostrum as a chairperson. Did you feel her presence giving you a calming influence and it was indeed her poetry given to you by the pen that you read out and the congregation so liked hearing. She says that there is no need for a meditation to bring herself and her father forward. He is the chief of the tribe they once belonged to so long ago. The necessary bonding from this world to yours and they offered themselves as gatekeeper guides and have chosen to be by your side until others are appointed to you. With regards to this particular bonding of your present gatekeeper (THE CHIEF), you have both bonded for quite a few lifetimes this being quite a rarer bond from this world to yours. He especially wants you to know this my sweet dear angel. Never question his influence in your life and the world will be your oyster.

May we say that you have a natural way with your earthly connections between one person and another endearing them towards you, and only when jealousies creep in that you feel threatened, so try and work on how to combat this feeling within. You asked for a contact with your Grandad here. We have to tell you that for a short while he will be on a higher plane of existence of which you played a big part in getting him there by sending your energy field towards him by thought on many occasions.

Now where were we? Oh! Yes. Now that the nicer weather is here, busy yourself outdoors for awhile darling as you get so much enjoyment planting out your bulbs and as spring approaches you'll see the flowers blossom and grow just like the special bond we have here for you. We have no seasons as you do and time is relevant only to that of which we would like to spend corresponding spiritually, if we so choose of our own making. You will find also when you ascend to this plane your evolvement will be of greater value due to all the spiritual links you have accumulated this time around.

My sweet child the longing you have to better yourself must grow and we will help you twofold. The spiritual body within you is crying out for this so go *along with the flow and our protection towards you will be paramount.*

Your family clan are gathering around you now just to say hello.

Firstly Auntie Ethel says please pass on her endearment to your Uncle Bob. Your Gran Goodacre wishes to send hers to her son Bob too. Also Evelyn is here to pass on a special thank you for the kindness and warmth of love you showed her when on the earth plane. May we say that the love you give out so freely, even to strangers entering your church for the first time is a guiding light that many should follow that you are creating for yourself sending plenty of family love around your birthday in October where invites going to family and friends will be sent, of course there will be no need to invite us as we take it upon ourselves to invite ourselves on such occasions. Don't be alarmed as we know how to conduct ourselves in public! You are the only one so far, to see us within your earthly circle of family and friends.

As we take our leave Auntie Helena wishes to be remembered, another conquest joining our happy throng here, with the love again unquestionable.

PRIDE AND GRATITUDE
IS FOR EVER YOURS
AND MAY IT ALWAYS CONTINUE TO BE SO!!!!

Love from The Clan and your present Gatekeeper Guides.
Xxxxxxxx

Dear Reader As you can see this script was full of many answered questions that I felt at the time. Firstly the energy that we give off when communication is held gives the recipient a larger auric field to which they can use this extra energy to enable them to go onto a higher plane of life within the realms of the spirit world and why when giving a reading to someone here on this side of life the recipient feels quite energised rather than depleted of the spirit found within all of us. Secondly I believe that slowly I was being introduced to some of the universal laws that exist governing us all on both spheres of life. It was also very nice that my efforts within church life had been noticed and was my destiny. I might add I held this office for quite some years.

When I left Hinckley Spiritualist church the committee and congregation presented me with a beautiful stone angel sat reading a book to pair up with an identical one that I had bought that week to take to Spain with us. The birthday celebration mentioned was to be my 50th which I was not looking forward to, and given this prompt I decided I would celebrate in style with a forties fancy dress party to be held at our local pub, an evening of which I have very fond memories. Sixty guests took part with all my family and friends rallying around to make the evening go with a bang and which I will tell you all about this later on in the month of October.

With regard to the stone angels, I remember my husband John complaining bitterly because of the weight and having to store them in a barn at a friends gite in France till we became settled. I insisted as they meant so much to me. I'm so glad I did as they now reside in a prominent place in my garden of 28,000 square meters of perfect scenery. I treasure this setting every morning and thank my spiritual leaders for choosing such magnificence to settle in that creates peace and tranquillity at my most precious times, so that I can produce this work for you. Also the comment from my father who was a keen gardener struck home that "Yes" at times I feel so revitalised when putting right the land surrounding this little place we call home.

Lastly I present to you the first quote of which I read out to the church's brethren given to me by Pancho, the daughter of my first gatekeeper guide:

When blossoms show and winds blow,
We know the earth is replenishing itself,
As the blossoms fall and new buds form,
This is how we also replenish ourselves,
From the essence of youth,
becomes the wisdom of the old,

May we stand up and be counted,
As there is more to life than at first we knew.
May we enfold the mighty oak tree with
our arms around its great girth,
And feel the pounding of its strength
soaring through our veins,
Till we feel strong again
"Thank you Mother Nature, for just being there".

Love P.

Script of 4.4.96 May we say there is always an interactive way of looking at things. We understand you are quite upset on the passing of Tom who was a parishioner of yours whom you sat with on many occasions. We know who you are talking of and he was known as a fine gentleman. No one here has heard of him coming to this realm yet, but he may be recuperating as it has only been a few days and his family here would wish to be with him at the moment. If we get the chance we will forward your regards on.

On occasions like this when there is a sudden passing there are mostly guiding lights of atonement to be reached which takes time but take solace in the fact that a sudden passing into this world of spirit is a blessing for the soul, do you understand? He will undoubtedly see you again doing your work in the church and maybe pass a message to you through a visiting medium, so don't shed anymore tears at his funeral of which we understand your church is holding for him. He had chosen this particular time to come back home to us and be with his spiritual family here. Being a practising spiritualist helped him in his latter years there so that his transition *will be quicker than some. If you get a chance tell his daughter who is quite knowledgeable on spiritual matters that there is to be no more grieving on his behalf. In answer to the question she has recently asked, there is to be an awakening for her which is about to happen and that mankind as a whole will know of it too as there is a fountain of knowledge being passed from one to another at this present time and by word of mouth. You will also become aware and will be involved with this. All will become clearer as time goes by.*

May we leave you with the fact that your psychic abilities are now at such a level of attainment that your primitive trance like state is not needed to link in with us and our higher beings when blending your thoughts to ours.

Our blessings go to you our sweet child,
Yours Truly, The Clan x
And your guiding light of today X

P.S. It is just filtering through that Diane is to receive a newborn into the family of a boy weighing 10lb 3 ozs.

Dear Reader Tom's funeral was the first spiritualist funeral I attended as the secretary of the church and the vast congregation showed what a lovely person he was. It also showed me what a lovely angelic service a spiritualist service can be where, within the address the minister and president of the church was able to subtly give personal messages to those left momentarily behind on this vale of life. This was delivered in such a sensitive way throughout the service taking care not to offend those who had different beliefs attending.

The next script came about with a break-in we had at our church where our speakers and P.A. system were stolen. These were replaced by my husband's surplus equipment which was not needed by his present band. This actually got him into our church for the first time rather spookily as he put it. He was fitting the new equipment, nervously looking over his shoulder occasionally, expecting something or someone to jump out at him as previously described in the Ian Paisley episode. A misconception that a lot of people have as spirit do not wish to alarm you and they have an ethical code or spiritual law to adhere to at all times, where their peers in spirit would admonish any entity not shown abiding by them. This episode was rather upsetting to our church committee and I felt that if spirit had such law and order on their plane of life maybe they could help to bring the perpetrators to justice by helping to identify them. We had had a spate of vandalism on the outside of the building for some time where some unruly youths thought they could evoke spirit to retaliate in some way.

Script of 25.4.96 *Yes! We are trying to help you, as long as you write what we are telling you! Be warned though that our attempts may be futile, after all who is going to believe you, but our blessings go out to you for your efforts.*

The first guy has blonde long curly hair on top and shaven at the back, large blue eyes with a wide open look. A wiry youth with sharp features, long thin nose and pointed chin with high cheek bones, pointed side burns, medium to small height, long fingers sporting many rings on them. He has a slight limp at the moment and acts like the leader of a gang.

The other guy is quite tubby with rosy cheeks, flaring red when he is loud mouthing off. A bulbous nose and furrowed brow, out of keeping for his age, short hair shaped with a crew cut standing on end and shaven at the back, brown eyes, wears a thick heavy chain around the neck, strong heavy shoulders he is a well built young man, he has grazes to his elbows from a previous exploit.

Lastly, a third youth, wiry with ginger hair, very tall, he has suffered a dislocation of the left shoulder and would have had to visit the local hospital for it, he is the oldest of the three with hair similar to the first youth mentioned, size ten shoes, he thinks he is a right villain and sports a tattoo to prove it. All three live in your locality.

There you are dear and the best of luck with whomever you may show this script to, but we will advise you that the young lady Police Constable has an open mind and is more approachable with this kind of evidence and being young she would dearly like to bring these to justice.

If you have success then may we help in the future with any other such dealings that come your way?

Before we take our leave of you may we affirm that our light is to shine brightly as you preach our way of life to others. Don't let any obstacles get in your way. Our divine leader is speaking to you and also wishes to impart that you have a strong self will. Use it often when being opposed by any that may wish ill of you where whatever you believe in strongly gets tested. You know when our teachings come through to you so strong, after all a true spiritualist will know instinctively where you are coming from, striking a cord with their likeminded beliefs. Let us say that when the time comes to stand up and be counted you will have learnt the most from our plane. Never let anyone try and enforce their ways and beliefs onto you that may guide you away from the true pathway. Stay within the boundaries set by your church affiliation with the Union until the time comes to be set free to go amongst the many peoples *that you will inevitably meet, with the philosophy coming quite naturally as we prepare you to be often linked into the higher consciousness.*

We offer you our abounding Love and Light
from all here including,
The Clan. XXXXX XX

Dear Reader This was my first liaison with spirit showing an astral influence with the earth plain on a more serious nature. The police force inquiry was drawn to a close more quickly, I feel, because of spirit's intervention with a speedy arrest and conviction. Finger prints had been taken at the scene at the time, having eliminating the fingerprints of our committee.

Script of 5.6.96 & 6.6.96 *Welcome to you dear Lesley, we are all here. It has been some time – where have you been? We are glad you have come back to us when you have more time today. We only got the pleasantries out yesterday before you had to leave us. Our moment in time can be suspended as it were, so that if a break occurs abruptly we can resume again as if this has not occurred. Our blessings go to all of you there and Grandad is here to say that he watches you often when drawn towards you when you are gazing at his photograph. You are considering joining the open circle at church and wish us to be there. Our leader here says it is not always possible for all of us to attend but we can send a representative.* **YES! I replied.** *Our aim is to please where we can and to impart the knowledge, which is vast with the emporium we have here. Your church foundations are only at their infancy at the moment as there is a lot for mankind to learn yet and our belief is well centred into your being, after many lifetimes spent there on the earth plane. No person can take your guiding light away from you however experienced they think they are at psychic ability your links to spirit will become stronger the more opposition you may receive from these people and we are talking from now on.*

We all love and respect you as we send all our love with a special hug from Dad x, your ever present leading Guide P. *Also The Clan xx*

Script of 13.6.96 *Hello Lesley to follow on from your previous text with us may we guide your shining light afield as it were and go forward six months from now. We see another term of office and we think you deserve this as the good you are doing must continue. On the home front Mum may find she's struggling a little to keep her faculties going, don't worry about her though she will cope as dad says he looks in on her regularly to get cursed now and again when she can't find something. Auntie Mable is also here today and wonders what she has discovered with regards to our little meetings here. We have invited her to our happy throng where we connect with your earthly vibrational link which amazes her. May we let her show that she is capable of holding a conversation with you by holding your pen?* **Yes, surely, I replied**. *God bless you Lesley. WOW! THIS IS NOT SO EASY AS IT LOOKS, I'LL HAND YOU BACK TO OUR LEADER.*

I see you have an old healing problem back so we will keep this short and afterwards our contact healing will be sent to you dear one.

Sarra's problems will increase then diminish as she has to find her own way without, forgive us in saying, being tied to your apron-strings. She needs to grow in a different way on a different level to yours. This situation she is finding herself in is self induced with a particular guidance of a sort. She has to go through certain trials and tribulations that she found in the past. There is a strong need within to find her desire to progress with a different approach to life. There is no need to worry as this is in hand with her grandma looking over her, along with her own guardian angel and the close knit family that we have always been. Your need is *ours. Blessings to all of you including Glen and his partner Sarah whereby a similar affect is going on that you will become alerted to at a different time.*

Human Life on your plane have a lot more impact than you think to do with progression onto this plane of life. We are eager to learn more and more about mankind's behaviour patterns. Your family here have proved this beyond a shadow of doubt. Control of all other forces outside this circle can not be tolerated so that you know your needs are given in truth. Do you understand this? I AM BEGINNING TOO!

Little do we know when we start on this spiritual pathway, that day by day we grow in the knowledge of our faith in human soul existence, may it be so. Always endeavour to give factual information as you receive it without embellishment, and we will be so proud of you. Of course as you have your own gatherings on a tutorial level this rule will be applied also.

Love as always your guiding light x

Dear Reader I felt that at this stage of my life and leaning on the spirit realm for guidance, the scripts given previously were immeasurably of use to me. Indeed, learning all the time how material everyday life with its ups and downs, and forever trying to be the best mum I could be with this insight, it was hard at times to stand back while my children sorted their lives out in the way they saw fit. I think that maybe we can all take a little of this virtue.

Script of 18.6.96 *We understand you have an administration problem at your church. May we help? We are gathered in force to debate your dilemma. We feel that as you were not strong in the beginning of office that the woman in question* deemed fit to challenge you and your officers of the church on a matter that has drawn the union's attention. She should have consulted with you in a formal way first but her aim was to get the presidential position by challenging Diane and yourself on a mundane matter and thought it would be a walkover. Dorothy is your best contact so make sure she is made aware of the full facts. We have faith in you darling. Soldier on with this without a fuss. You will find that you and Dorothy have something in common where if you give her a bone she will chew on it all day says one of us.

Our leader here says that all your hard work to date must not go to waste. We have laid this faith down for all mankind to adhere to and by all creation we will not let this fold, nor will the Union, once they learn all the facts by sending the union's legal representative. Keep your chin up and after this episode you will find a new bolder inner strength is born. Where can we ever get such good people all working together with the love and light you all radiate, please pass this onto your committee as this will give Diane the lift she needs right now. Show Dorothy as it will be deeply felt that you are all doing the works of the union and indeed have a spiritual bonding within the church, starting at the very top of your committee. You asked after Mrs. Hathaway who founded the spiritual church in Hinckley and what she thinks. She is present as our special guest and her thoughts on this matter are that she is behind Diane (her prodigy) with the running of the church on the earth-plane. She has a great regard in her efforts in keeping the church running in the way she had once done. Now taking the pen she writes WHATEVER KEEPS THE CHURCH

DOORS OPEN SO BE IT, BUT IT MUST BE FOR THE GOOD OF IT'S MEMBERS!!!! GOOD LUCK AND GOD BLESS! And so say all of us.

Our blessing to you dear daughter,
Love to you from The Clan. Xxxxxx
Your Guiding Lights of two. Xx

Dear Reader As you may have gathered there was trouble gathering at my then work place and my first serious one in office whereby a couple had tried to break up our present committee. They were of the lower ranks at the time with ideas above their station, trying to pass a miss-demeanour that I am not at liberty to divulge. Suffice to say it was done to try and shake our resolve with the smooth running of the church to the standard that the union lays down for all the churches throughout the Midlands. The outcome was most favourable with our statements being read out at the tribunal held at our church with the representative that spirit had forewarned me of. It also strengthened my bond with the head of the union's committee at that time.

A triumph indeed to which I send my humble thanks to those who helped us throughout this difficult period, both here and on the higher consciousness of life.

Script of 11.7.96 *Hello sweet child and welcome. We are here for once more nearly a month has passed by. We realise that it is John's birthday today; we will pass his regards onto his mother here and the rest of the Shepherd family. This pen is not very free flowing, take a short break and come back with another. Thank you, that's better. Are you comfortable? Then let's see what is on your bright horizon today. There are compliments galore with the strongest amongst us saying that there are never enough willing workers for your church, don't push yourself too hard in trying to step into too many* *positions because they are not filled. You will wear yourself out and we are sure that Diane is very grateful for whatever you wish to contribute. Never be afraid to ask where there maybe an element of doubt creeping into any given situation. Never mind making mistakes in the spelling, you must take this down as it flows and correct at the end as the teachings to others in the most natural way will be astounded by many both peers and pupils at this stage in your life. May we all join together in wishing you and yours well and to further your career without any more hindrance in this field. Proceed slowly till you feel your feet, as you do in most areas of your life and people will come to your way of thinking eventually, we promise.*

Let us all pray it does some good as there is enough badness in your world, just don't get hurt if someone is aggressive towards you as they may only be jealous of the goals you are setting which are just right at the moment, but we urge you not to take on any further commitments as this will stretch you too much. Never go out of your way for people, let them come to you not vice versa, enabling you to make the most of your given time.

Dad has just appeared and says that he is glad he made it before signing off so he can send his biggest squeeze and kiss from him.

Love from The Clan and your guiding light in spirit xx

XXXXX

XXX

X

Dear Reader The signing off of the pyramid kisses have always been the sign of my Mother in-law's presence. Further proof in the above text that my peers and family guide me through this way of life and are forever present through times when sorely tested.

Script of 27.8.96 *Hi welcome back to our fold, it has been a long time, your holiday being a great success. We are back with you with much to tell you about our plane with a willing communication to pass onto others as we speak of your church service tonight. May we say well done! People will be queuing up to hear what you have to say before long and we hope to be able to help convey many messages to your brethren such as:-*

Now the time has come to take stock of yourselves and what we know of this passage in time and where it is heading. Let us rejoice in what we achieve in this life and then in the next we can go forward with an upliftment of the heart.

Simplified, this means to sort out ongoing problems this life time around so that excess baggage is not carried forward to the next. Our blessings my dear child go to you with this pearl of wisdom presented to you, with many thoughts coming through to you in the future for other services from those here on this realm. A break is what you needed; look out for more offers of going abroad in the offing of a more conducive nature so that you can contemplate that given with many pleasant interludes. We see a holiday of a life-time coming up in the near future too. Next year maybe a move will take place which will take your extra resources up, but trust us and be patient.

We are most aware of Sarra putting out a distress signal and we have thrown her many options by pen, it is up to her now, as it is her individual input on her destiny to unfold for herself. Please pass this knowledge on to her if you get an opportunity to do so.

Go forward young woman even though your joints are beginning to ache with the onset of osteoarthritis. We are well aware with this form that finger work precision being is a work of love as you ride above the pain which is felt sometimes as this illness progresses through your body, but be rest assured that we will help you to cope without pain while working with us.

Love to you as always, the Clan and your ever present guide in spirit. XXXX

Scripts of 27.8.96 - 29.8.96 There is a very good philosopher here on this realm that wishes to link in with you on a permanent basis, is this alright with you dear? **YES!** Let it be so then! When he comes forward you will feel differently within your feelings of a vibrational link to us and you must write whenever this urgency is felt. In time you will begin to give that given in a different way than that of the past years where this form of communication has been channelled through to you, whether by pen or by voice communication. May we also say that your life is spanning out quite nicely at present making no shadows but true formations sixth sense wise, also making a few unexpected connections with Bridging Guides from other dimensions linking up with you for exciting channelling yet to come. This is coming about in the next few weeks as you seem to be impatient to forge ahead with a quickening happening within you at present which many are feeling at this present time as your earth plane approaches a new millennium of enlightenment. However, listen to John when he says you are getting obsessive when being passionate about whatever is going on in your working environment instead of your personal life, forgetting your own needs. This is your nature we know only too well, but he is right that you back off now and again and enjoy what life has to offer on a fun level, which we also know you are capable of. John realizes that he has neglected you and his family with his managerial duties taking him away from home time after time leaving you to cope for many years. He is doing his up most to make amends now, just as you have found solace in the church.

Dad has just popped in as he has a concern regarding your mother's welfare. We have conveyed to him that there is no need to worry as everything is going to her wishes, she only has a short span left there ON THE EARTH PLANE and they will be re-united one day with no suffering when she takes the higher side of life. He has promised to take her hand in his as they pass through to this veil together. We will all comfort you and yours when this happens. Let us close now with this comforting knowledge. This knowledge is easily given to you but alas not too many others, but hopefully though through the written word this will change many attitudes for the better.

LET EVERY DAY PASS WITH THE KNOWLEDGE
THAT COMES SO EASILY, YOURS TO PASS
ON WITH THIS MESSAGE:
LET ALL MANKIND BE FOREVER GOOD TO ONE
ANOTHER AND LET PEACE REIGN THROUGHOUT
THIS PRESENT TIME IN PASSING.
LET US QUALIFY THAT:-
WE KNOW OF THE PASSING YEARS AND
OF THOSE TO COME, THESE WILL BE

CRUCIAL TO MANKIND.
LET THIS BE SO!
NEVER LET IT BE SAID THAT WE DO NOT CARE.
"WE DO" AND FURTHERMORE ALL OUR LEADERS
HERE ARE MOST CONCERNED AS TO WHAT IS
HAPPENING WITH YOUR EARTHLY PLANET.
THERE HAS BEEN A HOLOCAUST AMONGST YOU FOR
A NUMBER OF YEARS, ALL BE IT STREWN
FROM DIFFERENT HEMISPHERES.
WE KNOW OF THE TIME WHEN THIS WILL END.
THIS IS WHEN MANKIND WILL COME TO TERMS
WITH THEIR FATE IN THIS MATTER.
THE KNOWLEDGE IS ALREADY WITH YOU AND A
CHOSEN FEW WILL BE AWARE AS TO WHEN.
IF YOU HAVE BEEN PRIVY TO SUCH
INFORMATION AND ARE READY TO
SERVE BY FOLLOWING THE INSTRUCTIONS
GIVEN THEN PLEASE, PASS THIS ONTO
OTHERS OF THE SAME MIND SET
WHICH HAS BEEN GROWING IN
NUMBER AMONGST YOU AS WE SPEAK.
END.
THIS IS BEING GIVEN TO YOU BY ONE OF YOUR
BRIDGING GUIDES, WITH LOVE AND LIGHT.

We are now back with you Lesley and we are glad that you found the above enlightening enough to push you into many walks of life.

Such links of the higher consciousness have long been awaiting you and we have been so pleased with your efforts to master a certain higher frequency for this to happen, our blessing to you on this achievement which in our eyes you were ready for a long time ago. We never push anyone along a certain pathway though, we just bide our time and *eventually each mortal brings themselves along to a certain attainment. We also work with John's thoughts when we are not able to forcibly link with your-self.*

The cottage we talked about is still in the offing. He will push for this, he is more aware of his destiny than you think.

Dad says he will never let you down; you are the most precious thing to him still. May we say it goes both ways as we feel the strong bond you have between the two of you.

Our leadership here is the finest you could wish for Lesley so press on with this given pathway. The world is your oyster with regards on all matters.

Best Wishes from the Clan including Dad xxxx

And Your special guides today xx

Dear Reader With regards to my previous scripts, I recall my friend Pam asking me recently what pushes me on to enlightening others with the circles held today and many seminars under my belt. She was I believe trying to protect me from the attitudes of others taking my business away from me. I also feel that rather than taking my business it enhances it with the help I offer others, enabling them to act on their ideas, encouraged by me and also passed on by spiritual connections. I personally feel that they are not a threat but an equal. I encourage a loving mutual respect to flow between us as I strongly feel we cannot put ourselves any higher than that of the ordinary person walking our streets as they chose to either feel spirit with them, or to ignore those feelings of the higher side of life living amongst them.

These scripts make me feel so humble whilst basking in their vast knowledge, as you will also be made aware upon receiving such knowledge and I hope you will have the conviction to do something about it and becoming a more fulfilled person.

Script of 30.8.96 *Hello once again my darling child and what do you wish of us today? We are still looking out that special abode for you. We are more aware now of the urgency as your sale is impending. It will present itself out of the blue as your other property did. Be rest assured that everything is being done in its own time. May we add looking for you is a pleasure; we have so much fun and debate here when we are asked on our progress on such a pleasant task. Not such a chore for us as we have many spiritual eyes only too willing to be looking around for you. Please link into spirit when walking inside to look around a property and you will instinctively know if it is right or wrong for the both of you. Just to recap, we think you are looking for pleasant surroundings to suit your artistic talent and good neighbours to bond with.* 'YES.' *We look forward to the challenge.*

Now to your enlightenment, our prophesy today is not to dwell on the bad things in life but to go forward to the future in an eloquent way that everyone knows you have been there. Good eh!!! Always keep laughter in your life Lesley as this is your best feature. Remember as you give this take some for yourself.

Picture yourself sat in an open field with nature all around you with your art pencils drawing away in the most peaceful way, this is how we see you and know so well. Retire from the rat race now and again for awhile as this will replenish your batteries to enable you to take on other duties that life throws at you. We know it is a struggle to be nice all the time when meeting so many people but you do it so well and so eagerly. Let the storms roll with us at your side for ever there to guide you through them. You have been over the biggest hurdles now so sit back and let others go on their own journey of life.

Your guides here say that you are one of the brightest pupils they have come across for some time, so please don't spoil it on earthly trivialities.

We have a saying that THE MEEK SHALL INHERIT THE EARTH!!!

We are almost out of time today. Let us pray that

everything comes up to your expectations and remember, only you can make certain decisions, a freedom of choice whether of good or bad that goes for all mortals on the earthly plane. We step in when your thoughts invite us to do so! So trust us with the inevitable advice given. We are aware that you like the best life has to offer and why shouldn't you! When another asks you to relinquish this way of life don't, as you would be so miserable. These spiritual feelings are in the core of your being and have been for many lifetimes, and you and I will know each other for some time to come.

Your Ever Loving Guiding Light X

P.S. The Clan are resting today. Forgive us as we knew you needed higher guidance.

GOD BLESS!
Mum in-law
XXXXX
XXX
X

Script of 9.09.96 *Hi darling, we know you only have a short while with us tonight but welcome, my sweet. We have important news for you. Within your new circle at home you have a very lucky lady as she is well prepared. Yes you are correct in assuming Jan, she will some day become well known in her own right due to you and your insight of leadership and pointing her in the right direction. Our leader here says thankyou as we may not have known her capabilities without your intervention. Are there more of your prodigies? Oh dear you are ailing, that is why the short time. We can feel your respiratory system as we speak and will endeavour to help you my love.*

All is well on this plane as we hope on yours. We hear that his lordship is back and we must close for now. Get in touch shortly please as we have more to offer.

Dear Reader Janice and I met at church and had become firm friends. She then came along to my home circle and already had good instincts and was very enthusiastic. After a period of time she began to run her own circle and gave seminars at the local colleges, she also had open days at her home of which I was happy to attend.

Script of 12.09.96 Hi again, your guide is here and a few others are present as well, what knowledge can we impart today. Firstly that important phone call is coming where your home buyer is concerned as the market has improved and we still foresee a wonderful place for happier times and time to reflect on your happiness together. *We can see a pleasant journey ahead for the both of you. Evaluate more of what you want and go for it. We will endeavour to show you the way from here on in.*

We bring tidings of a new member coming into your fold where Luke is going to have a brother. Blessings to Tara and Mick they will also move when a sister will come along, we know the joy for the whole family as we bring this knowledge to you from this higher realm, behold another one to fuss over.

We send a little philosophy:-

FROM THIS REALM TO YOURS
BEHOLD SUCH A WEALTH OF DREAMS
NEVER TO BE TOLD SO FACINATINGLY
AS YOU ARE NOW TO HOLD THE VERY KEY
TO YOUR EVOLUTION.

Blessed are those who once they take the reins to this realm pull on them to stride forward into the unknown.

There are such treasures to be found. We momentarily escape from our lives to live others for them, we do not perish; our thoughts are that this will bring happiness to others who cannot see for themselves. Our blessings go out to the teachers that they may teach the blind.

The meek are to inherit the earth, most definitely. OUR OWN TEACHINGS HERE ARE TO FOLLOW THOSE WHO WE KNOW TO BE TRUE BELIEVERS IN SPIRIT FORCES. And you are one of these people. Let us pray that you impart our knowledge to the best of your ability. We know you will always treasure this way of life as you were brought back to do our bidding in this way. The fields of knowledge we will bring will enhance your life enormously. Let us say you will become quite famous in your field. Look to the future prospects with pride, be sensible as where we belong here is a pleasant existence so create this peace of mind and you will do well. Liken yourself to a prodigal son or daughter - sorry - simply there will be an awakening of the soul. There are lessons to be learnt here, pleasant ones of course. You will feel so much more contented with life which you have not felt for some time you know! We are doing our level best to get you there my darling so put all your faith in us!!!!

Nonsense will be talked about how we exist but you will know better as you have learnt well. Sarra will indeed also be happier as she relearns the pathways we have given her from the beginning similar to your own. A belonging is the key to both of your happiness feeling right. This level of consciousness has to be looked into by your good-selves. Linking in with spirit with eloquent words is not always enough so do be patient for things to become clearer before questioning them.

Become more knowledgeable and impart this knowledge. We welcome this. Believe in your dreams.

Evaluate them as you experience them, take heart that you are right in your interpretations of them and eventually no thought will be ever questioned. Where spirit entities are concerned, like attracts like, and the expertise will be given, and there is never a more important time than the time you are living at present. So go forward with a smile on your face and love in your heart even if you are thinking that things are so bleak, there is always another bright and sunny day. Only do what you can do and no more my sweet however be forever vigilant that you are doing your best to keep the status quo and no more, hence feeling poorly when you over do things where the church is concerned.. We think that is enough for today.

God Speed, all our love to you and yours for ever from The Clan and your advisors from this realm.

Dad, Mum In-law and your guiding light. XXX

Script of 15.09.96 *Hi there, we all send lots of guidance today, the pleasure is all ours may we say! Look forward to the month of May next year for everything to solve itself where your children's problems will disappear and they settle with new partners for life so stop worrying. Level your commitments out so that you're not rushing around and be yourself for once. Take that mask off which you show the public and friends as there are more things on heaven and earth to do, so do it. This is your time, not your children's. Because you care for them so deeply they are scared not to disappoint you by doing the wrong thing by sorting their love-lives out, and feeling a failure. Let them be free to make their own mistakes from time to time. Be careful to follow your* *pathway to your dreams instead, looking towards the happiness you can share with your loved ones rather than the despair of others. We see that you are too easily drawn along this path. It is dangerous to your health Lesley. We are always watching over you and we know what is best for you at this time. Pleasant things are going to awaken your spirit in such a way there will be no going back.*

Dear Reader I would like to share with you one of the said moments of above where, while John my husband was playing in his band, our friend Ray and I had been jiving quite hectically. I felt him pull me over to look at the beautiful scenery of the coast line where the gig was being held and the view was spectacular as the sun was going down around the harbour. Simply from one artist to another budding one, he said to me, just look at that, and for that split second we both felt the inspiration that natures created picture can bring, and a feeling of utter contentment flooded over us with all the people milling around us that just didn't exist. A precious moment in time, one of many as my life progresses with our world in the here and now forever changing.

I also have put the above scripts together as the links seemed to be telling me that my life was beginning to take on a more tutorial route with successful home circles, psychic teas, and personal readings. Also avid reading of the many books loaned to me by the parishioners and friends of the church spurred me to share my thirst of knowledge with others in this new field. A minefield of general information but not backed up in the usual way. I take care to run such information before my constant spiritual guide querying authenticity in what I read on varied subjects such as soul expansion and retrieval, Aura fields and the hierarchy of the different realms from the angelic field to the gatekeeper philosophy, healing and bridging guides you are issued with when reborn and how the expansion of these guides help to determine which are appropriate on given situations as your pathway forward enfolds, giving straightforward facts encompassed in my dear reader anecdotes. From 1997 towards the 2000th year I was leaning towards a higher state of consciousness with a fine tuning of the vibrational energy the body emits when allowing the higher entities from spirit world to connect with me. I have chosen to put this material into a further publication naming this work ***A Diary Through Spirit Intellectually*** where my bridging guides of another interplanetary existence, having asked permission of the higher realms of this world before connecting with me, have peppered their scripts with their philosophies, wisdom and views of how they can help with furthering the ways of mankind and steering them into a brighter new future.

I leave you with my Gran and Grandad taking a stroll as I would like to take you to our next book.